Illustration: Magali Lefrançois.

Susanna Moodie, 1803-1885.

Anne Cimon

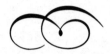

Anne Cimon is a Montreal literary journalist and poet. Her articles and reviews have appeared in such publications as *Books in Canada* and the *Montreal Review of Books*. Her interest and research in nineteenth-century literature is reflected in her articles and inspired a series of poems in her book *No Country for Women* (Mosaic Press, 1993) on the nature writer Henry David Thoreau.

She received her Bachelor of Arts degree from Concordia University in 1993 with a Specialization in English Literature. In 2002, she won a prize from the Writers' Federation of New Brunswick for her essay on the Canadian poet Irving Layton whom she studied with. Her first book *A Skin of Snow*, a collection of poetry and prose, appeared in 1981 when she lived in Toronto. She has published two bilingual books that reflect her French heritage: *All We Need/Tout ce qu'il faut* (Borealis Press, 2002) and *An Angel Around the Corner/ Un ange autour du coin* (Borealis Press, 2004).

In the same collection

Susanna Moodie

Library and Archives Canada Cataloguing in Publication
Cimon, Anne

    Susanna Moodie: pioneer author

    (The Quest library; 28)
    Includes bibliographical references and index.

    ISBN-13: 978-1-894852-19-7
    ISBN-10: 1-894852-19-2

    1. Moodie, Susanna, 1803-1885. 2. Frontier and pioneer life – Ontario. 3. Ontario – Social life and customs – 19th century. 4. Authors, Canadian (English) – 19th century – Biography. I. Title II. Series: Quest library ; 28.

PS8426.O63Z62 2006   C813'.3   C2006-940992-7
PS9426.O63Z62 2006
Legal Deposit: Fourth quarter 2006
Library and Archives Canada
Bibliothèque nationale du Québec

XYZ Publishing acknowledges the support of The Quest Library project by the Book Publishing Industry Development Program (BPIDP) of the Department of Canadian Heritage. The opinions expressed do not necessarily reflect the views of the Government of Canada.

The publishers further acknowledge the financial support our publishing program receives from The Canada Council for the Arts, the ministère de la Culture et des Communications du Québec, and the Société de développement des entreprises culturelles.

Chronology: Clarence Karr
Index: Darcy Dunton
Layout: Édiscript enr.
Cover design: Zirval Design
Cover illustration: Magali Lefrançois
Photo research: Anne Cimon and Rhonda Bailey

    Printed and bound in Canada by AGMV
    (Cap-Saint-Ignace, Québec, Canada) in October 2006.

XYZ Publishing
1781 Saint Hubert Street
Montreal, Quebec H2L 3Z1
Tel: (514) 525-2170
Fax: (514) 525-7537
E-mail: info@xyzedit.qc.ca
Web site: www.xyzedit.qc.ca

Distributed by: University of Toronto Press Distribution
5201 Dufferin Street
Toronto, ON, M3H 5T8
Tel: 416-667-7791; Toll-free: 800-565-9523
Fax: 416-667-7832; Toll-free: 800-221-9985
E-mail: utpbooks@utpress.utoronto.ca
Web site: utpress.utoronto.ca

International Rights: Contact André Vanasse, tel. (514) 525-2170 # 25
E-mail: andre.vanasse@xyzedit.qc.ca

MOODIE

Susanna

PIONEER AUTHOR

XYZ
Publishing

To Eileen,
and always,
my family

The Visionary Woman who is intuitive and sees into the future
reveals messages – sometimes dark prophecies, sometimes
visions of light – and is suspect to the rational mind.

– Linda Schierse Leonard, *Meeting the Madwoman*

Contents

Quebec City, lit by an autumnal glow, appeared as a shrine to Susanna from the deck of the ship she had been on for nine weeks.

Prologue

A Strange Land

> I felt that I was a stranger in a strange land;
> my heart yearned intensely for my absent
> home. Home! the word had ceased to
> belong to my *present* – it was doomed to live
> for ever in the past; for what emigrant ever
> regarded the country of his exile as his
> home?
> – Susanna Moodie, *Roughing It in the Bush*

Susanna, unable to stay in the dank interior of the cabin, had come back on deck for some cool air and a last look at the panorama of Quebec City. She stood tall and straight at the railing of the brig *Anne* and watched as the moon rose and cast mysterious gleams upon the landscape. Towering pine trees seemed to frown down upon the St. Lawrence River, which flowed rapidly between rugged banks.

How could she possibly find words to describe this sublime landscape? And yet she felt a familiar pressure, the desire to capture it on paper for others to experience. At twenty-eight, Susanna had left London a well-known literary figure, and she had copies of her first volume of poetry in her luggage. She had married John Dunbar Moodie a little more than a year ago, on April 4, 1831. Now they had a baby, and like hundreds of emigrants from Scotland, Ireland, and Britain who filled the ships anchored in Quebec harbour, they were seeking a better life in the colony of Upper Canada.

The *Anne*, jammed between other vessels in the crowded harbour, had suffered serious damage during the night when a larger ship accidentally plowed into its deck. Many of the passengers were awakened by the loud noise and rushed up to see what had happened, Susanna among them.

"What's all the confusion?" Susanna inquired of Captain Rodgers. Surrounded by a group of women who had become hysterical with fear, he couldn't speak.

"Let the poor man alone," Susanna exclaimed, "We must go below deck. We'll be safer there."

The force in her voice convinced the dozen or so women to follow her. Susanna hadn't allowed her own fears to show.

"Let's pray," she suggested.

One young woman cried that she didn't know how to pray.

"Just repeat the words after me."

And Susanna had begun to recite the Lord's Prayer.

~

Now, a towline had been attached to a huge steamer, which began to tug the *Anne* out of Quebec harbour. Enveloped in black smoke and flinging red sparks out of its funnel, the steamer resembled some fire-breathing demon. Susanna stood at the railing of the *Anne* and struggled with her anxious thoughts. *Will we even reach our next destination, the port of Montreal?* she wondered.

In the darkness she felt like a pilgrim, her head filled with visions, her fate in the hands of Providence, as the ship carried her up the river into a strange new land.

Thomas Strickland purchased the Elizabethan manor Reydon Hall
in Suffolk when Susanna was five. She liked to hide in the attic
to write stories with her sister, Catharine.

1

Country Girl

I am the creature of extremes, the child of
impulse and the slave of feeling.
— Susanna Moodie, *Letters of a Lifetime*

S usanna Strickland was born on December 6, 1803,
in the village of Bungay, Suffolk, England. She was
the sixth daughter of Elizabeth Homer and Thomas
Strickland. She followed Eliza, Agnes, Sarah, Jane, and
Catharine Parr (named after the sixth wife of Henry
VIII). Born sickly, Susanna was quickly baptized at St.
Mary's Anglican Church, for her parents feared the
worst. Her given name had a tragic connotation
because the name recalled Susanna Butt, Thomas

Strickland's first wife, who had died while giving birth. Her brothers, Samuel and Thomas, followed, to complete the Strickland family.

For a child with a poetic temperament like Susanna, rural Suffolk was an ideal place to grow up in. Only a few kilometres away in the Lake District, William Wordsworth and Samuel Taylor Coleridge were leading the Romantic Movement with their *Lyrical Ballads*. First published in 1798, this volume would later influence Susanna deeply.

At three years old, Susanna played with her sisters and brothers on the grounds of Stowe House, a Georgian manor Thomas Strickland rented in the Waveney Valley. The setting was Edenic: Susanna often ran to the stream and cupped her hands to drink the pure water, or pulled wild strawberries from the bushes to eat her fill of the sweet fruit.

She soon accompanied her father and her older sister Catharine to the Waveney River, which looped around the village of Bungay. Fly fishing was her father's favourite sport: Susanna watched her father from the green bank as he waded into the water with his fly fishing pole. *If only I were as pretty and sweet as Catharine*, Susanna thought, as her father talked to her sister. *If only I had the same long blond hair, and not these red curls that no comb can tame.* Catharine was the favourite; everyone in the family knew that.

"Father," Susanna cried out: "I've seen a crocodile."

"Now, Susanna, be quiet. I must concentrate."

Her father shook his head at his youngest daughter's imaginative ploy and continued to fish. Susanna didn't know how to be any different. She could only be herself. She was more like her brother Samuel than like Catharine, for whenever she saw a frog leap in the grass, she tried to catch it with her bare hands. She didn't like her dolls; she wanted to keep a frog in her bedroom.

∞

Susanna's father hoped country living could heal his gout. The chronic disease inflamed the joints of his hands and feet and kept him in bed for weeks in excruciating pain.

Thomas Strickland was born in London and grew up in genteel poverty. He was ambitious, and as a teenager he found employment with a well-known London shipping company, Hallet and Wells. Thomas's favourite mottoes, which he passed down to his children, were "God helps those who help themselves" and "Persevere and you must succeed." He advanced quickly in the firm, became a manager, and eventually owned properties.

In 1808, when Susanna was five, Thomas had made enough money to purchase the attractive Elizabethan manor Reydon Hall, a country retreat located about one kilometre from the coast of the North Sea. Reydon Hall, with its many rooms and its mullioned windows to look out from, was where Susanna put down roots that tugged at her till the end of her life.

Thomas Strickland was ahead of his time: he believed that his daughters ought to be educated. Elizabeth gathered her girls in the parlour every day to teach them not only sewing and crafts, but history, mathematics, even Greek and Latin. Susanna, like all her sisters, developed a passion for reading. In her father's library, she took any book she liked, even those from the collection that had once belonged to Sir Isaac Newton, who had been the great-uncle of Thomas's first wife. On winter evenings, the family gathered before the warming flames of the fireplace in the library and listened to Agnes, who adopted a very regal manner as she recited favourite passages from Shakespeare or her own compositions. By the time she was nine years old, Susanna was writing her own poems filled with gloom and grandeur as well as tragic plays with larger-than-life heroes like Napoleon.

One cold afternoon, despite their fears of Old Martin, the ghost the servants warned them against, Susanna and Catharine climbed to the attic garret. Now imaginative girls of twelve and thirteen, they had discovered an old trunk with brass hinges that was reputed to have belonged to an Indian prince.

"Let's open it!" Susanna, her grey eyes flashing, coaxed her younger sister. "Maybe there will be clothes, or even jewels, to wear."

They lifted the heavy wooden lid and found something even more precious: paper – reams of paper – that expensive commodity they never had enough of for their scribblings.

"Let's write a story right now," Susanna suggested. "I have so many ideas."

Catharine agreed. Close together in the dusty, dim place, they each started to write a story. At times, the silence was broken as they excitedly read passages to each other. Suddenly, Eliza, their eldest sister and the most severe, burst in on them:

"What are you two doing?" she asked sharply. After skimming a few pages, Eliza grumbled:

"This is trash!"

Susanna was so angry she picked up her manuscript and ran down the staircase to the nearest fireplace, where she threw the pages into the flames and watched, fuming, as they turned to ashes.

The Strickland children's daily life was idyllic, except when their father's gout worsened in the icy drafts of winter. Then Susanna and her sisters and brothers had to obey the servants while their mother nursed their father in the bedroom. Only Agnes had permission to enter: she read the newspapers to Mr. Strickland, who wanted to keep informed about London politics. Susanna often stood outside the door to listen, wishing she, and not Agnes, were the one by his bedside.

In May 1818, Thomas Strickland died. His health had deteriorated after an unwise loan to a friend cost him most of his business. Reydon Hall was left to Mrs. Strickland, but there was very little capital to provide an income for the family and they could hardly afford food.

Susanna, fifteen years old, grieved the loss of her father, whom she later described as a "good and just man," a "vigorous and independent thinker." In the first few months after his death, she was haunted by memories of her childhood misbehaviour. She'd close her eyes and see her father seated at the head of the dining table. Her sisters and brothers sat respectful and silent as Mr. Strickland announced in a bitter tone that Napoleon had escaped Elba. They all knew how he despised England's enemy. But Susanna couldn't help herself and let out a whoop of glee. Unlike her father, she admired Napoleon.

Why, Susanna asked herself now, *did I do such a bad thing? Why did I upset Father when he was not well?*

She was impulsive by nature. Yet her family loved her warmth and generosity. *How can I help Mother keep Reydon Hall?* Susanna wondered.

A friend of the family had taken one of Catharine's children's stories to a London publisher. To their great surprise, the story had sold quickly. Susanna had an idea for a tale about another hero of hers, the Roman gladiator Spartacus, and his exploits.

Maybe I can sell a book too! Susanna hoped. *And I might earn enough money to travel to London one day.*

2

Bluestocking

I have been one of Fancy's spoiled and way-
ward children... I have studied no other volume than Nature, have followed no other
dictates but those of my own heart, and at
the age of womanhood I find myself totally
unfitted to mingle with the world.
  – Susanna Moodie, *Letters of a Lifetime*

After Thomas Strickland's death, Reydon Hall
remained the family home, but barely. The servants were let go, the ornate carriage sold, and a general air of decay infiltrated the scantily furnished
rooms, the unused attics, the empty barns and sta-
bles.

Portrait of Catharine by Cheesman.
Catharine was only a year older than Susanna and was her
"dear and faithful friend." She married and emigrated
to Canada the same year as Susanna did.

Weakened by her grief over the loss of her father and sensitive to the dampness and mould in the house, Susanna fell ill with whooping cough and became so thin she wrote to a friend that she looked like a "perfect skeleton." The usual medical recommendation at that time was "a change of air." But how could Susanna go anywhere when there wasn't even enough money to buy clothing?

Aunt Rebecca, who lived in London's Bloomsbury district, came to the rescue. She invited Susanna, and her sisters, to stay with her. Aunt Rebecca was a second cousin to their father, and a wealthy widow. She had been married to the architect Thomas Leverton, who had designed the fashionable Bedford Square where Aunt Rebecca lived.

At sixteen, Susanna liked to mingle with and pour cups of tea for the literary women known as "bluestockings" who often gathered in Aunt Rebecca's living room to discuss the latest books.

In 1826, Susanna stayed for several months at another London address, on Newman Street. Her sixty-year-old cousin, Thomas Cheesman, asked her to be a companion to his niece, Eliza. Cheesman was a sort of Renaissance man and amateur artist who became a father figure to her. He encouraged Susanna, and also Catharine, when she visited, to write.

One afternoon, Cheesman, or Cousin Tom, as the family called him, stared at Susanna as she entered his studio, where paper and paint cluttered the table, and the raw smell of turpentine filled the air. He remarked:

"You look particularly fetching, today, dear. Sit down. I would like to do your portrait. I must capture those red curls for posterity."

Susanna couldn't refuse. In fact, she did feel pretty in her new yellow jacket with its rolled collar and the string of pearls around her neck. She had even clipped a yellow ribbon in her auburn hair.

As she sat for the miniature oil portrait, Susanna was thinking, as she often did then: *If only my father were still alive. I miss him so.*

When Cousin Tom allowed her to look at the portrait, Susanna felt surprised at how he had been able to capture the sadness and apprehension that she tried to hide from everyone.

∞

Back in Suffolk, Susanna continued to recover from her illness. She loved to ramble in the countryside, away from Reydon Hall. She now knew that she preferred the country to the city. She sought inspiration for poems in nature. Her favourite outing was to the North Sea where the salt air cleansed her lungs and cleared her thoughts. Her appetite had returned as a result of her long walks.

One afternoon she relaxed on the beach, her picnic basket empty except for the remains of her lunch of apples, cheese, and bread. She recited out loud to the gulls swooping overhead her favourite verses from the book everyone raved about, Byron's *Childe Harold's Pilgrimage*:

> Are not the mountains, waves, and skies, a part
> Of me and of my soul, as I of them?
> Is not the love of these deep in my heart
> With a pure passion? should I not contemn

All objects, if compared with these? and stem
A tide of suffering, rather than forego
Such feelings for the hard and worldly phlegm,
Of those whose eyes are only turned below,
Gazing upon the ground, with thoughts which
dare not glow?

Susanna wanted to be one of those people whose thoughts dared to glow, and she hoped, as the waves curled and broke on the pebbly beach, that she would meet a man as passionate and soulful as Lord Byron, a man she could share all of herself with, someone who would travel the world with her.

Susanna overcame her isolation not only by reading her favourite authors such as William Wordsworth, Robert Burns, Sir Walter Scott, and William Cowper, but by immersing herself in an exchange of letters with her new literary friends. One of her most important correspondents was a local man named James Bird, known as the Bard of Yoxford.

One morning, before her walk, Susanna sat at her desk in her bedroom and pondered how to respond to the verses Bird had sent her for criticism. She didn't like their style. How could she express her true opinion without hurting Bird's feelings? Soon her pen was scratching onto the blank sheet of paper her candid answer:

"You are most happy in your descriptive scenes and I care not for Story in a Poem. I know most of Scott's descriptive scenes by heart while I scarcely remember his stories... Descriptive poetry often goes so home to my heart that I cannot read a beautiful drawn scene of this kind without weeping."

Susanna's high spirits came through. Tongue-in-cheek, she wrote,

"Mama is busy gardening and more interested in housing her potatoes for the winter than the blue stocking fraternity in composing sublime odes or entering the joys or sorrows of some imaginary heroine..."

∞

Being a heroine was the goal of Susanna's elder sister Agnes. Upon the death of Queen Charlotte, wife of King George III, Agnes had written a eulogy that was published in a London newspaper, and this immediately had opened doors into the aristocracy for her. Agnes often stayed at Aunt Rebecca's house but didn't think it was grand enough, according to Susanna. Her sister was theatrical and imperious by nature, and cared too much about her appearance.

The two rival sisters often visited friends together. Susanna, unlike Agnes, never put on airs, and joked about their being "poor poets." They even had to borrow the neighbour's donkey to pull their chaise, for they didn't have any other way to travel.

On one memorable evening, Susanna and Agnes returned from visiting the Birds in the village of Yoxford, about an hour away from Reydon Hall. The night was clear and the stars twinkled as the donkey, which Susanna affectionately referred to as "our mouse-coloured Pegasus," plodded down the road.

Susanna pulled her cloak tighter and squeezed close to Agnes. They were both silent, Susanna lost in thoughts about Samuel, their younger brother, who had recently emigrated to Upper Canada. A friend of the family had talked the destitute twenty-year-old boy into trying his hand at farming. Samuel's letters were filled with marvellous descriptions of the wilderness and exotic place names such as the Otonabee River.

"Agnes, do you ever long to join Samuel in Upper Canada?" Susanna asked, breaking the silence of the night. "It seems like such a romantic place."

Susanna didn't have to wait long for an answer as she felt her sister stiffen beside her on the seat.

"O no, never," Agnes blurted. "I only dream of living in London."

As their chaise pulled in at the tollgate, clouds suddenly formed and the air turned cold. In the semi-darkness, Susanna spotted a vagrant man who was hiding behind some bushes. Suddenly the man let out an unearthly scream.

"Someone's tearing at my veil!" Agnes shrieked as she clutched the flimsy material, though she later admitted she had only imagined this.

Susanna laughed whenever she recounted this nerve-tingling incident, which she wanted to include in a story for a gift-book anthology. She hoped to make her own mark and distinguish herself from her flamboyant older sister. She was gaining confidence as a professional writer and didn't like the fact that their shared family name sometimes caused confusion. She wrote to Frederic Shoberl, the editor of the gift-book anthology, *Ackermann's Forget-Me-Not*, on June 3, 1829, to clarify a matter:

"My sister and I seldom communicate our literary business to each other, as our friends in the world of letters are often of different parties and totally unknown to each other, but I am sure Agnes is too honourable ever to have demanded payment for me, without apprizing me of her intention."

∞

Catharine was another matter altogether. Susanna had grown so fond of the sister closest to her in age that she remarked in an undated letter to the writer Mary Russell Mitford, that she would prefer giving up her pen rather than "lose the affection of my beloved sister Catharine, who is dearer to me than all the world – my monitress, my dear and faithful friend." Susanna had sent one of her poems to Mitford, who had responded with compliments. From the Berkshire area, Mitford was sixteen years older than Susanna and had gained critical and popular recognition with her five-volume *Our Village*, a collection of rural sketches.

For the time being, Susanna busied herself writing and publishing children's books. These earnings helped their mother make ends meet. She shared with Catharine the friendship of Laura Harral, daughter of Thomas Harral, the editor who published their stories and poems in the gift-book annual, *La Belle Assemblée*. Susanna received much praise when her story "Old Hannah: or, The Charm" appeared in 1829. In a bold fashion, Susanna sketched a story about the Strickland family's old and cantankerous servant Hannah, who had entertained her with tales of ghosts and magic since she was a child. The fledgling author had created her first memorable character based on a real person.

∞

In the summer of 1830, Susanna, now twenty-seven years old, lived in London as a guest at the house of Thomas Pringle and his wife Margaret. Susanna had been "adopted" by Thomas Pringle, who edited a popular journal and had published her works. She referred to him often as "Papa" in letters to friends at that time.

As a young man, Pringle had emigrated to South Africa and edited a newspaper for many years until his controversial views against the institution of slavery cost him his livelihood. In 1827, he returned with his family to live in London where he became the Secretary of the Anti-Slavery Society. Aware of Susanna's compassionate nature and writing ability, Pringle asked her to transcribe, or ghost write, the story of Mary Prince. Prince was a forty-year-old woman born in Bermuda, who had been a slave in the British colony of Antigua and was now sheltered in his house.

Susanna sat on a chair in Thomas Pringle's study and wrote down the horrifying experiences Mary Prince, who insisted she wanted to stand rather than sit, described in her singsong voice:

"I can show you my scars, Miss Strickland," Mary offered.

Susanna's throat clenched. Could she refuse? No. She wanted to see the evidence for herself.

"I'll help you," Susanna said, seeing Mary struggle with her blouse.

Susanna stood behind Mary and gingerly lifted the cotton blouse and undergarment.

"Mary, how could they?" Susanna exclaimed, as she stared at the rounded back with its crisscross of embossed black flesh, glistening in the bright light of the lamp on the desk.

"They did that to most of us," Mary answered matter-of-factly.

Deeply shaken, Susanna sat back down on the chair and continued to record Mary's story. Mary had been malnourished, had suffered beatings, and worse, had been raped by her owners, who were supposedly upstanding Britons. How could this be? Susanna now wanted to shape the story into an unforgettable document so that people would learn, as she had, of the evil that was slavery. The pamphlet was published anonymously in 1831, with an introduction by Thomas Pringle, as *The History of Mary Prince, a West Indian Slave, as Related by Herself*. It sold quickly and was reprinted three times. All the profits went to "Black Mary," as she was affectionately called by the Pringles.

Susanna also accepted a commission to write the story of Ashton Warner, another former slave befriended by Thomas Pringle. Warner was twenty-four years old, and in such poor health that he died before the pamphlet was even printed.

Susanna's social conscience was awakened by these dramatic encounters. She resolved that she would no longer be an accomplice to the criminality she had recorded. She poured her outrage into several poems that were published in journals and eventually in her first book, *Enthusiasm and other Poems.*

That same summer, Susanna met someone else at the Pringles, someone who would change her life forever.

Portrait of Susanna by Cheesman.
In her youth, Susanna's grey eyes often expressed the sadness
she felt at the sudden death of her father, "a good and just man."

3

Enthusiasm *and Love*

...there is to me a charm in literary society
which none other can give...
– Susanna Moodie, *Letters of a Lifetime*

Susanna's poetry had many admirers in London, and
in her own neighbourhood of Suffolk. In fact, she
had found a patron in Andrew Ritchie, the pastor of the
Congregationalist Church in the village of Wrentham,
about two kilometres north of Reydon Hall. She had
joined the small village church in April, a few months
before leaving for London and the Pringles' house.

Suffolk was a region of dissenters, especially local
farmers and poorer families. They rebelled against

what they perceived to be the moral laxity of the Anglican clergy, who seemed to prefer fox hunting to attending to their flock.

Susanna loved the chapel, one of the first "independent" chapels ever built. The setting was romantic with its beautiful lane of fine old trees and meeting yard full of lilac bushes and laburnum. Susanna had a favourite spot where she imagined she would be buried one day: under two pines through which the wind sighed a lullaby.

Mrs. Ritchie offered to teach Susanna how to paint, and they sat outside, choosing the prettiest flowers to sketch on paper. This skill Susanna used often to relax from the demands of writing and publishing.

On the night of her formal admission to the congregation, Susanna had been soaked to the skin by lashing rain as she travelled to Wrentham from Reydon. Her decision to join the Congregationalist Church had shocked her Church of England family to its roots. They had refused to accompany her, though that had not changed her mind.

Pastor Ritchie, her spiritual advisor and friend, came up to her in the vestry where she stood alone:

"Are you ready, dear?" he asked, offering his arm like a father ready to take his daughter up the aisle to give her away in marriage.

"Yes" she heard herself say with more conviction than she felt.

Susanna stood in a pew opposite the pulpit. The assembly was seated. She liked the rugged features of the farmers and their wives, mostly poor folks who gazed at her. She trembled from head to foot. Every eye was on her.

Susanna buried her face in her hands, and tears wet her fingers when Pastor Ritchie recommended her as a new member. But during the last beautiful prayer, her spirit revived. She rejoiced that the ordeal was past and she was now a member of a "free church."

∞

On the morning of August 12, 1830, Susanna sat at the dining table at Reydon Hall, grudgingly slipping flyers advertising her first book, *Enthusiasm and Other Poems*, into envelopes addressed to friends and acquaintances. She didn't like to have to do this but that was the agreement she had made with a London publisher, Smith & Elder. She had to raise enough money by advance sales of her book to cover the cost of printing. Orders for fifty books had already been filled, but she needed to sell a lot more. *Who can I possibly turn to next? Who would know a lot of people interested in poetry?* Susanna asked herself.

In a flash, the name of Mary Russell Mitford, whom she had never met but corresponded with occasionally, came to her mind. Hadn't the famous writer praised all the poems she had sent to her? Susanna now felt more cheerful and immediately reached for her pen and a fresh sheet of paper. After a few pleasantries, she swallowed hard and came to the point:

"Will you excuse the liberty I am taking, dear Miss Mitford, in enclosing the prospectus of a small volume of poetry which a friend of mine has undertaken to publish for me by private subscription? I should feel greatly obliged to you if you would circulate them among any of your wealthy friends who are unfashionable enough to be lovers of poetry..."

Whenever she could, Susanna liked to use humour to sweeten the way. Miss Mitford responded positively. By year's end, Susanna gratefully held her first volume entitled *Enthusiasm and Other Poems*, an elegant, plain leather-bound book embossed with gold. The forty-seven poems expressed her religious faith and her romantic love of nature. On May 28, 1831, Susanna happily read in the leading London magazine *Athenaeum* that *Enthusiasm* possessed "a tone of tender seriousness which marks a refined and reflective mind."

∽

John Dunbar Moodie was a prized guest at the Pringles' London home in the summer of 1830. "What brings you back to us from South Africa?" Thomas Pringle inquired as they shared a drink in his study. His eyes were shining with pleasure at seeing his friend, after eleven years apart.

"I need a wife to help me on the farm," John had shot out, his honesty always bracing. "I'm afraid I'm becoming too much of a hermit."

Moodie was a Scot, from the Orkney Islands, and at thirty-three years old, he had a lame arm due to an injury suffered while fighting in the Napoleonic Wars. He'd emigrated to South Africa soon after the war in the hope of earning quick money, but that hope had been dashed. As a retired officer on a small pension, Moodie had little to offer a wife, yet deep in his heart he knew there was someone for him. His trip to London had another purpose: to find a publisher for his manuscript of African tales, mostly about hunting wild animals.

At the Pringles', Moodie regaled their feisty red-headed boarder, Susanna, with his anecdotes. Susanna, tall and thin, didn't mind that John was short and stocky, for he had thick hair that framed a face she thought noble. She liked that he was a writer and that he openly admired her poems, which she gladly read to him.

John fascinated her. She looked forward to the evenings, when he would play his flute after their meal with the Pringles. Sometimes he invited her for a walk on Hampstead Heath, where they lingered under the shade of the ancient oak trees. On a walk in the early autumn, under a cool blue sky, John was deep in thought. Then he turned to her and asked tenderly:

"Beloved Susie, would you marry me and come to South Africa?"

Susanna shivered, from the cool breeze and from excitement. These were the words she had both dreaded and dreamed of hearing. She was tempted to marry John, whose chivalrous and poetic nature she had come to love in such a short time, but she didn't want to emigrate to South Africa. She couldn't imagine being near the leopards, elephants – and worst of all, the snakes – that John hunted around his farm. She loved John more than anyone, except perhaps Catharine, but she had some thinking to do before she gave her answer.

∽

Despite her fears, Susanna soon accepted John's proposal of marriage. He immediately left for Scotland to meet with relatives and request inheritance money to help support a bride. John was a member of the gentry, but his estate, Melsetter, had gone bankrupt.

Left alone, Susanna began to doubt whether she would be able to bring herself to emigrate to the faraway farm. She'd thought she could be happy anywhere with John, whether beneath the burning sun of Africa or building a nest among the eagles of the storm-encircled Orkneys, but by January 1831, Susanna chose to break the engagement by sending a "Dear John" letter. The Pringles, and other friends like James Bird and Reverend Ritchie, counselled Susanna not to abandon her writing career in London. They reminded her that South Africa was a colony where slavery, which she abhorred, was legal.

Susanna rented a back room in a house five minutes from the Pringles. To keep the rent affordable, she had to share the room with Miss Jane Jones, an acquaintance of the Harrals. Susanna pursued the literary life and was herself pursued by men who admired her for being a published poet and author of lively reviews and articles.

By the time John returned to London, Susanna had grown tired of the rounds of parties and agreed to meet with him. When John declared that he had given up any plans to live on his farm in South Africa because he wanted to stay near her, Susanna was overjoyed. She accepted, without any more doubts, his second proposal of marriage.

∞

On April 4, 1831, Susanna and John were married in a modest ceremony at St. Pancras Church in London. The guests had first gathered at the Pringles' house. A wedding breakfast was served, and then Mr. Pringle helped Susanna into the carriage, which whisked them to the steps of the church.

Susanna missed her father, who should have been the one to give her away. She had insisted her mother and sisters not travel to London for the short ceremony as she wanted only Catharine as her bridesmaid. "Black Mary" was also present, in a brand-new dress.

At the altar, John anxiously awaited his bride. He feared Susanna might change her mind at the last minute, but he was reassured when he caught a glimpse of her. She smiled at him saucily and thought, *John looks very handsome in his wedding suit.*

The organist began to play. Mr. Pringle offered Susanna his arm and then led her down the narrow aisle. Her bouquet of white roses and lilies of the valley sweetened the air. Catharine, holding back tears, followed close behind. She was feeling vulnerable because her engagement to Francis Harral had been broken. However, she did approve of John Moodie as her sister's choice.

Susanna spoke the sacred vows. When she stated "the fatal obey," as she referred, tongue-in-cheek, to the traditional Christian promise of the wife to love, honour, and obey her husband, the tears that shone in her eyes were not from regret, but from joy.

∞

"My blue stockings, since I became a wife," Susanna joked to James Bird, in a letter dated April 9, 1831, "have turned so pale that I think they will soon be quite white, or at least only tinged with a hue of London smoke."

By August, Susanna, now pregnant, wanted to be near her mother and sisters. John found them a cottage near Reydon Hall in the village of Southwold. It was close enough that her family could walk over every day.

Soon, a visitor arrived. Thomas Traill, a boyhood friend and fellow officer of John's, was a widower. Susanna liked him. He had studied at Oxford and loved to read. Whenever Catharine was in the room, Thomas seemed to be so cheered by her that Susanna encouraged her pretty, sweet-natured sister to visit often. But Susanna had more to keep her busy than matchmaking. In late February, she gave birth to a baby girl promptly named Catherine, later Katie for short.

Now that she and John had the baby's future to consider, how could they better their financial situation?

John attended the popular lectures on emigration to Upper Canada, which were given by a certain William Cattermole. Cattermole was a huckster who described the young colony in his talks and pamphlets as a paradise where people could expect to prosper easily. Thousands of desperate British citizens followed the carrot he dangled before them. John was accompanied to these lectures by his friend Tom Wales, a younger man from a wealthy background who wanted to emigrate to Canada. Susanna and her sisters, who knew Tom Wales, found this funny.

Susanna would later describe Tom in her book *Roughing It in the Bush* as "a man in a mist, who seemed afraid of moving for fear of knocking his head against a tree …a man as helpless and indolent as a baby."

When John asked him if he was qualified for a life of toil and hardship, Tom answered back:

"Are you?" and added prophetically: "Gentlemen can't work like labourers, and if they could, they won't. You expect by going to Canada, to make your fortune, or at least secure a comfortable independence. But the refined habits in which you have been brought up, and your unfortunate literary propensities, will make you an object of mistrust and envy…"

Another visitor to Reydon Hall dismissed Tom's unattractive description. Robert Reid was a well-to-do settler in Upper Canada and father-in-law of Susanna's brother Samuel, who was also doing well in the colony. Reid, who had ten children, charmed the family with his Canadian anecdotes and promises of wealth. Retired half-pay officers such as John Moodie were eligible for grants of free land, and this became the final selling point. Susanna's brother would take care of securing land for the Moodies near his own, while the couple made their preparations to emigrate.

As the time for their departure drew near, Susanna became despondent.

The prospect of leaving her friends and native country was so intensely painful she couldn't sleep. The woods were bursting into green leaves and the meadows and hedgerows echoed with the song of birds and the humming of bees. *To leave England*, Susanna mused, *is dreadful – to leave in Spring is doubly so*.

∽

On May 13, 1832, Susanna and John attended the wedding of Catharine and Thomas at St. Margaret Church in the village of Reydon. The whole family was in attendance, despite the fact that Mrs. Strickland didn't approve of Thomas, and neither did Agnes or Jane, who were bridesmaids. They saw only a tall, balding, impoverished widower, nine years older than their beautiful kind Catharine. But Susanna saw Thomas differently. As she watched him gently slip the gold band onto Catharine's finger, she sensed that he truly loved her sister, and that alone was what mattered.

And Susanna had another reason to rejoice in the wedding. Catharine and Thomas had decided to emigrate to Canada. Thomas had attended the lectures by William Cattermole along with John and had been convinced of the benefits of leaving England as soon as possible. Susanna wouldn't be separated from her favourite sister after all.

As Agnes and Jane stood by Catharine's side at the altar, they couldn't understand how she, like Susanna, could choose to go to a far-off colony where there were no theatres or libraries and where their homes would be made of crude materials.

4

The Crossing

Parties of emigrants and their friends were
gathered together in small picturesque
groups on the pier. The cheeks of the
women were pale and wet with tears. The
words of blessing and farewell, spoken to
those near and dear to them, were often
interrupted by low, pitiful wails, and heart-
breaking sobs.

– Susanna Moodie, *Flora Lyndsay*

On June 2, 1832, Susanna, the baby Katie in her
arms, and Hannah, the teenage servant, stood
beside John on the deck of the steamer bound for
Edinburgh, Scotland, where they would board a ship to

In 1832, Grosse Isle near Quebec City had become a quarantine station, where all ships sailing to Canada had to stop for inspection, including the *Anne*, the ship Susanna Moodie was on. She never forgot her visit there.

Canada. They were leaving Southwold on the North Sea at the tail end of a powerful storm, and Susanna squeezed her arms even tighter around Katie as the wind whistled around them and the waves lashed the sides of the boat. She was already nauseous, seasick. How would she survive six weeks on the Atlantic Ocean?

Tears welled up as she remembered saying farewell to her mother at Reydon Hall. Would that be their final embrace? Would she ever return to Reydon Hall and see her family again?

She had to remind herself that she had a new family now: John, standing so stoic beside her, obviously excited to be on another life adventure; her beautiful baby, Katie, sleeping against her chest; and Catharine, and her new husband, Thomas Traill, who were already on their way to Upper Canada, the dreamed-of land of opportunity.

☙

Susanna spent the night pacing the deck. At dawn, she saw a beautiful city rise before her. The captain, who teased her for not having her sea legs, growled as he passed by:

"Mrs. Moodie, Edinburgh is a fine sight, but Quebec City is just as fine!"

"You've made me happy!" Susanna replied. Now that they were approaching the rocky Scottish coast, she felt excited and well again.

The news, when John inquired at the dock, wasn't good: their ship had already sailed and they would have to find another one bound for Canada. John decided they should go to the nearby port of Leith where they could stay with friends.

In Leith, they were warmly welcomed and entertained to the point that Susanna thought if she weren't British, she would like to be a Scot. Susanna enjoyed the daily walks with John down the cobblestone lanes in search of another ship. She didn't want to leave on the *Flora*, the ship John preferred, as she found it unsanitary. One morning they saw a posting for the *Anne*, and Susanna convinced John this was their ship because the captain had offered them a cabin, a rare privilege. Despite the fact that there would be a two-week delay before the departure date, the Moodies paid the fare.

Cholera was spreading throughout Europe and had reached the coast of Scotland. When Susanna fell ill with a high fever she feared that she had contracted the deadly disease. After a week of rest in bed, she rallied enough to be able to board the *Anne* on the afternoon of July 1, under gloomy storm-tossed skies. As the ship sailed past the rugged Orkney Islands, John proudly pointed out his ancestral home, Melsetter.

Several weeks into the voyage on the Atlantic, the *Anne* began to feel like a prison to Susanna. John, who enjoyed travel and wasn't seasick, kept busy trailing a fishing line or exchanging stories with Captain Rodgers and his crew. Susanna nursed the baby while trying to get Hannah to do the chores. Already Hannah was becoming rebellious as she anticipated her arrival in Canada, where she'd heard servants could better their lot.

They were making good time and Captain Rodgers had decided not to stop for fresh provisions. This decision proved to be a mistake, for soon the passengers' food had to be rationed. The rationing was severe: oatmeal, morning, noon, and night, with a few spoonfuls of port wine. Bored in the confines of the cabin, Susanna began writing a story she entitled "Noah Cotton" and read excerpts aloud to John, but she couldn't keep up the strength to finish it. She felt too ill with hunger even to nurse Katie.

The *Anne* was stranded for ten days along the Grand Banks because there was no wind to fill the sails. Gigantic icebergs loomed out of the fog and frightened Susanna as she stared dejectedly out of the porthole.

In the last week of August 1832, the *Anne* sailed into the Gulf of St. Lawrence. The delicious scent of pine wafted through the ship, refreshing the fetid air. At Cap Rosier, a local captain came on board with provisions of water and food for the passengers, along with some unsettling news: cholera had now spread to Canada. The ship would have to make a stop at Grosse Isle, a quarantine station twenty kilometres before Quebec City, to be inspected for the disease. Only the Moodies would be spared this ordeal for they were cabin passengers and not considered a health risk.

∞

On the afternoon of August 30, 1832, Susanna, cradling baby Katie in her arms, sat beside John in the small boat that would take them ashore. She couldn't believe she would at last step onto firm land after nine miserable weeks aboard the *Anne*.

Grosse Isle appeared to be an earthly paradise to her despite the ominous tents and sheds of the quarantine station. The sight of the many whitewashed farmhouses comforted her, and the glint of the sun off the tin roofs of the churches lifted her spirits.

As John helped her out of the boat and she stepped onto the rocks that had been heated by the sun all day, Susanna cried out in pain. She felt as if flames were burning the soles of her feet through her worn-out shoes.

What she saw next, past some low bushes, shocked her sensibilities: hundreds of men, women, and children, most of them Irish, all steerage passengers from the ships at anchor, were shouting and yelling as they bathed half-naked in the river. Many were washing their tattered clothes, scrubbing them against the rocks and laying them on the bushes.

Am I in Babel? Susanna asked herself as harpies – rough, sunburnt women – rudely jostled their way past her and the baby. Noticing Susanna's distress, John took her arm and led her to a wooded path he had discovered.

"Let's take this path. We should be able to find a place away from here to rest."

John led the way through the woods, and when they came upon a shady nook at the edge of the rushing river, they sat down. Though Susanna could still hear shouts and yells, she felt safe, as she ate some hazelnuts and wild plums from the bushes to alleviate her hunger pangs. The air was hot, and mosquitoes swarmed around baby Katie, who cried until she was red as the setting sun.

The captain came for the Moodies and told them the boat was ready to take them back to the *Anne*, where they would feast on fresh provisions of bread and butter, beef, and onions. Susanna, who had longed for such fare for weeks, couldn't wait to get back on board the *Anne*, which no longer appeared a prison to her.

On September 2, the *Anne* sailed into the port of Quebec City. Susanna had been on the crowded deck of the ship for several hours. The stunning panorama surpassed anything she had ever seen in Britain. An autumnal glow lit the fortress city that jutted from the steep banks of Cap Diamant and reflected in the deep waters of the St. Lawrence River. Susanna felt as if Quebec City was a shrine and God was very near her.

She had an intense desire to visit the city but John persuaded her not to. Only he went in the boat with a group that had been warned by the captain about the danger of the cholera. Susanna could hear the church bells in the city tolling for the dead.

"It's a filthy hole." Susanna heard some passengers say when they came back on board hours later. John, thankfully, was among them. Some did not return.

"He is dead! He is dead!" A young Irish woman shouted, when she didn't see her husband among the passengers.

She crumpled onto the deck, hugging her child against her cadaverous chest.

"My dear Tam, the pestilence has seized upon him; and I and the puir bairn are left alone."

Susanna bent down and gently touched her shoulder barely covered by the ragged dress:

"Your husband will be back. He'll surely catch up with us in the next port. Have faith!"

Susanna felt the anguish of the frail young mother as if it were her own. Wouldn't she have felt such panic if John hadn't returned? But he was safe now, below deck with baby Katie.

∞

Upon their arrival in Montreal, the Moodies rented a room in the Goodenough Hotel, which Susanna found luxurious after the cramped cabin. They had agreed on a change of plan. Rather than continue their voyage on board ship, where a case of cholera had been diagnosed, they would take a stagecoach to Cobourg, their final stop.

As she rested on the bed, Susanna wished she knew how Catharine was. Had her sister and brother-in-law arrived safely in Canada? Susanna couldn't know that a few weeks earlier, Catharine and Thomas had rented a room in a hotel nearby. Catharine had been stricken with cholera but had survived, mainly due to the selfless round-the-clock care of the hotel staff.

5

Rough Canadians

Our hut is small and rude our cheer,
But love has spread the banquet here…
– Susanna Moodie, "The Sleigh-Bells"

In September 1832, the Moodies arrived in Upper
Canada with high hopes to find a place in literary
society. When they settled into Cobourg's Steamboat
Hotel, Susanna picked up the *Cobourg Star* and excitedly noticed that three of her poems and a story by
John of his African adventures had been published.
She remembered that Mr. Reid had offered to submit
their works to the local editor. Now their names would
be known. Hoping to meet kindred spirits, Susanna
introduced herself to the women at the hotel.

Despite her primitive life in the bush, Susanna found the will
to write and publish in Canada. She also bore several children.

"Yes," one plain-faced lady told her: "I know you write books, but we don't want a Mrs. Trollope in Canada."

Susanna didn't know who Mrs. Trollope was. She learned only later that she was the British author who had satirized American society with her acerbic pen. Another woman exclaimed, "I am glad that I can sew a shirt and clean my house, rather than write. It's not a useful occupation."

Among the strangers at the hotel, the Moodies saw a familiar figure. Their friend Tom Wales greeted them warmly and generously offered them his room because the hotel was full for the night. Susanna and John were disappointed when Tom announced he was returning home to England. He had contracted the ague, a form of malaria, and had no more money to live on. Eccentric as ever, he was taking home with him a bear he had adopted and kept in a shed.

When, the next day, Susanna and John met the bear nicknamed Bruin, they exchanged a look that Tom intercepted. He remarked jokingly:

"Yes, there is a strong resemblance; I saw it when I bought him. Perhaps we are brothers."

Tom had begun to caress Bruin, who growled at him.

"He's my only Canadian friend." Tom added.

∞

In the uncomfortable back rooms of the hotel, Susanna spent hours alone with the baby, while John went on daily excursions to look for a farm near Cobourg. After much input from Susanna, who feared the wild beasts in the forest, he had decided that it would be wiser to stay close to the village.

While Susanna tended to Katie and waited for John to return, she suffered acutely from homesickness, which she referred to as a "malady." The walls of the hotel were thin, and her sobs were overheard. There was a knock at the door. Susanna, desperate for company, didn't hesitate to open it. She recognized the petite Canadian woman who was staying with her husband at the hotel:

"What! Always in tears?" the woman exclaimed. "This constant repining will never do."

"The sight of you has made me feel better already," Susanna answered. She admired this woman, who was neatly dressed, as Susanna had noticed most of the women in the colony were.

Susanna confided:

"If it were my decision to make, I would be off by the next steamboat for England."

The woman answered: "You will like it better by and by; a new country improves upon acquaintance."

Susanna couldn't agree yet with that statement, but the woman wanted to discuss another matter.

"I need your help, Mrs. Moodie," she said, her face now serious. "There is a young Irish man who is near death in another room. He requests someone to read the Bible to him. Would you be willing to do that?"

Susanna, who had an evangelical disposition, agreed immediately. She was eager to be of service, and her faith gave her strength.

After three weeks of searching, John purchased a farm on eighty hectares of land, five kilometres from Cobourg. The price was exorbitant, but John believed the investment would pay off because the land was already cleared and was in a good location. One hitch was that the Moodies would not be able to move into the farmhouse but would have to live in a small log house, until Joe Harris, who had gone bankrupt and lost the land, could relocate his family of eight children.

Susanna, with Hannah and baby Katie, arrived first at their new dwelling, after a bumpy and rainy trip through the forest. John followed in another wagon with their belongings and Tom Wales, whom the Moodies had persuaded to stay in Canada and live with them on the farm.

Susanna was appalled at the sight of their new home. It was no more than a shack tucked at the bottom of a valley among dark woods. The driver, who was a Canadian Yankee, as British Loyalists who'd escaped the American Revolutionary War were called, cracked his whip and said sarcastically to the women:

"'Tis a smart location that and I wish you Britishers may enjoy it."

"You must be mistaken," Susanna replied. She was soaked by the rain, and trembling from the cold. "This is not a house, but a cattle-shed, or pig-sty."

Susanna was shocked by what she heard next, for she was still not used to the rude manners of some of the locals.

"You were raised in the old country, I guess," the driver responded, "you have much to learn, and more, perhaps, than you'll like to know, before the winter is over."

Black stumps of trees surrounded the shack, which had no door. Three young steers and two cows had made themselves comfortable on the dirty floor and had to be shooed out by the driver. There was only one window with a broken pane of glass, and not a stick of furniture to sit on. All there was by "some freak of fortune" was a pinewood cradle for Katie.

Susanna and Hannah were left to fend for themselves as the callous driver refused to wait until John and Tom Wales arrived. The two very different women were united in audible disgust for Canada, which seemed the worst place in the world to be in.

At least that was what Susanna felt until John, ever her knight in shining armour, appeared and made the situation seem less dire with his optimism and determined actions. They proceeded to clean the dwelling as best they could, unload their belongings, and light a fire in the hearth.

∞

Within a few months, Susanna was pregnant again. Despite her uncomfortable state, she had to continue her "distasteful chores." These chores were backbreaking, and what was worse, Hannah had left the Moodies' employment to find more remunerative work in the town, as many servants did once they arrived in Canada.

Susanna had to constantly wash clothes, bake, tend to little Katie, and fend off unpleasant neighbours like the Seatons – "Yankee savages," who would borrow something every day, from whiskey to tea, with the promise to return it, though they never did.

Homesickness weakened Susanna's spirits, especially at night. She would lie on the bed and hear the stream that ran nearby; in its deep wailings and fretful sighs, she fancied herself lamenting for the land she had left forever. John suffered the same pangs, and the couple drew closer together.

Susanna found some humour in the strange names of the shabby colonists. One evening, as they rested by the fire, she remarked:

"John, I find the names of people here rather odd. What about Solomon Sly, Hiram Dolittle, Reynard Fox? I wouldn't be surprised to meet Judas Iscariot, Pilate, and Herod one day."

Tom Wales, who was staying with the Moodies, wasn't much help because he was so ill. Emaciated and shaking with the ague, he took to a corner of the cabin to recuperate. Susanna knew Tom suffered from the diet they had to endure, which was mostly salt beef and pork and unleavened cakes. What could she offer him that would restore his strength? Susanna wondered. Bread! She could make a loaf of bread from a recipe borrowed from Mrs. Harris. The recipe was given without much graciousness, and Susanna found it somewhat complicated, but eventually she had made her first "Canadian loaf."

"What is that horrid smell?" Tom cried out from his corner. "Do open the door. I feel sick."

"It's the bread." Susanna replied.

She lifted the lid of the oven: "It's all burnt."

Her eyes were smarting from the thick smoke.

"It smells as sour as vinegar." Tom snapped back. "The black bread of Sparta."

Susanna had placed the loaf on the table, and when Tom sliced into it, the knife came out covered in raw dough.

"Oh, Mrs. Moodie," Tom said, "I hope you make better books than bread."

∞

Susanna was "making a book." Whenever she could, she jotted down her observations on bits of wrapping paper and receipts. She was determined to record her life as a pioneer and transcribed unusual conversations and descriptions of remarkable events and people. She read her work aloud to John, who was also writing poetry and stories whenever he could.

John was finding out that being a farmer in Canada was far different from what he had experienced in South Africa, far more backbreaking, especially as he was now older. And the money they had brought with them was disappearing as fast as snowflakes in the spring. Emotions were raw and morbid in the Moodie home. Susanna held back tears as John read her his newest verses:

"Oh, Let me sleep, nor wake to sadness
The heart that, sleeping, dreams of gladness;
Loved scenes, arrayed in tenderest hue,
Now rise in beauty to my view:
And long-lost friends around me stand,
Or, smiling, grasp my willing hand.

Again, I seek my island home;
Along the silent bay I roam,
Or, seated on the rocky shore,
I hear the angry surges roar."

John left her often to go by horseback to Cobourg, where he collected groceries and – even more valuable – news-filled letters from England.

One snowy evening, as she anxiously waited for his return, Susanna sat in the doorway of the hut and composed an upbeat lyric she entitled "The Sleigh-Bells." She mailed it off, with a few others, to the editor of the *Albion* magazine in New York City. In her cover letter dated February 14, 1833, she noted these were "the first flight of my muse on Canadian shores." She added boldly:

The close confinement of a log cabin, and the cares of a family, though they engross much of my time, have not been able to chill those inspirations, which in my own beautiful and beloved land were a never failing source of amusement and delight. The little sympathy which such feelings can meet with, in a new colony, where every energy of the mind is employed to accumulate wealth, has made me anxious to seek a more liberal channel of communication with the public, and I know no one to whom I can better apply than to the Editor of a Journal, which finds its way into the study of every respectable family on this side of the Atlantic, and is not inferior in literary merit to any publication of the same class in Great Britain.

To her great surprise, the lyrics were published. Susanna's ambition to become a professional author in Canada rose from its dying embers into a bright red flame.

∞

A letter from Agnes, from home! This was sweeter, meatier than any real food, for Susanna was famished for family news. She devoured the letter and wondered why she had ever left London. Agnes boasted of her successes, how she was published in the best journals and met the cream of society. She was even making enough money to support herself.

Susanna had confided all her troubles to Agnes in her last letter. She had described, as best she could, the isolation and burdens she had to bear, but as she reread the response from Agnes, Susanna realized that her elder sister didn't comprehend her desperate situation. Agnes suggested that she and Catharine, who lived two days' travel away in the bush, could edit a "penny magazine" together to make money. The idea was ludicrous, especially as there was little literary material in the colony to gather. *If only I could visit Catharine!* Susanna thought longingly. Ironically, she learned of Catharine's daily life from Agnes's letters. In the bush, Catharine had borne her first child and was struggling with poverty just as much as Susanna was.

And now Tom Wales had decided to return to England. There was no longer anything the Moodies could say to change his mind. How would they live without a friendly face from home?

∞

In June 1833, Susanna gave birth to her second daughter and first child born in Canada. She named the baby Agnes after her elder sister. The birth took place in the farmhouse, which the Harris family had at last vacated.

At first, mice had run everywhere and a dead skunk had been found in a cupboard, but the farmhouse was clean by the time Susanna went into labour, attended by Dolly, a local midwife.

Susanna soon returned to her chores. She learned to milk the cow without any fear. She often joked to John as she brought in the brimming pail to the kitchen:

"I'm prouder of that milk than any author of her best poem or story."

Susanna was learning new skills, but it became evident that she and John couldn't manage the farm alone. John decided to hire a couple to share the workload, and then the harvest. This was a common way of doing things in the colony, but the couple they hired proved to be dishonest. They stole the Moodies' food and farm tools and left them without supplies for the winter months ahead.

John noticed Susanna's spirits were extremely low. He feared she might go mad like a few of their neighbours, one of whom had even tried to take his own life. Providence intervened in the form of a generous legacy from Aunt Rebecca Leverton, who had passed away in London. They now could afford to return immediately to England with money to spare, but instead John took a trip into the bush seven kilometres north of

Peterborough, in Douro Township. He wanted to have a look at the parcel of land that was allotted to him as a British officer, land close to both Samuel Strickland's and Catharine and Thomas Traill's properties.

Upon his return, Susanna was won over by John's enthusiasm and agreed to his plan. They would sell the farm, pay their debts, and use Aunt Rebecca's legacy to build a brand new house on cleared land by the beautiful Lake Katchewanooka. Susanna was thrilled at the thought of living within walking distance of Catharine, though she knew she would have to overcome her fear that wild beasts might leap out at her from the forest.

∞

In the spring of 1834, the Moodies moved into their cedar log cabin in Douro Township. They named it Melsetter after John's ancestral home in the Orkney Islands of Scotland. Much of Susanna's homesickness was alleviated by her proximity to Catharine. Her sister's optimism and appreciation for the beauty of the Canadian forest were beneficial.

In the evening, Susanna sat by the window of the cabin to watch the reflections of moon, stars, and waving trees in Lake Katchewanooka. John purchased a canoe, and Susanna soon learned to paddle just as gracefully as the Mohawk and Chippewa women who lived in the camps nearby.

Susanna visited a First Nations camp with Catharine and made friends there. They gave her the name *Nonocosiqui*, which meant "hummingbird," though she thought the name was ridiculous for a tall woman. She soon learned that it referred to her love of painting these small birds.

One afternoon, she was invited into a wigwam and was offered what she called "Indian hotch-potch," a bowl brimming with a malodorous mixture of duck, partridge, muskinonge, venison, and muskrat smothered in onions, potatoes, and turnips.

As gently as possible, she pushed the bowl away from her:

"I am not hungry," she said to the elderly First Nations woman, "thank you."

She enjoyed their imagination but not their food.

In 1835, John's dream of publishing a book came true. The London firm of Richard Bentley printed his collection of hunting adventures entitled *Ten Years in South Africa*. John proposed another book, this time about being a settler in Canada, but Bentley didn't think it would sell. Years later, the publisher would change his mind when he read Susanna's manuscript *Roughing It in the Bush*.

In January of 1836, Catharine published *The Backwoods of Canada* with another London firm, Charles Knight. The book was a collection of her letters home, which Agnes had edited. Its leaden subtitle was "Being the Letters from the Wife of an Emigrant Officer, Illustrative of the Domestic Economy of British America."

The modest lump sum Catharine was paid for the manuscript didn't go far to alleviate her family's poverty. Though *The Backwoods of Canada* was printed in several more editions, she didn't make more money.

Susanna herself was gaining some fame, if no money, in the United States. *Enthusiasm and Other Poems* had been reviewed in the *North American Magazine* edited by Sumner Lincoln Fairfield. His praise had been of the highest, setting Susanna among the best-known women poets of the period such as "the celebrated Hemans, Baillie, Norton, Jameson, Howitt and Shelley, in England."

From the cabin in Douro, Susanna sent Fairfield a candid letter dated January 23, 1835. She thanked him for his appreciation and enclosed a signed copy of her book, as well as some new poems. She added humbly that she couldn't afford to send him anything more, as she didn't have money to pay for the postage. This admission of poverty was not made up. The Moodies had used up their legacy to pay for tools and hired help, and the land was not yet productive.

When John went to Toronto on business that first summer by Lake Katchewanooka, he left strict orders that the field hand, a surly, obstinate young man named John Thomas, should not fire the fallow until his return. This dangerous procedure involved setting the brush around the house on fire to further clear the land.

The day was hot and dry. Susanna, heavy with her third child due in a few weeks, sat inside the cabin at noon with the servant Mary. They worked on making sunbonnets while the children, Katie and Agnes, napped. Mary smelled the smoke first. By the time Susanna ran to open the door, she couldn't see beyond three metres. Flames encircled them.

"Who could have set fire to the fallow?" she asked out loud. The answer stood before her: John Thomas.

"O, ma'am, I hope you will forgive me," he confessed. "We can't get out. I've set fire in fifty different places."

He entered the cabin and Susanna quickly shut the door. Mary was whimpering and John Thomas began to cry. The children mercifully remained asleep.

Susanna knew the only "ark of safety" was the cabin. There wasn't even a way to get to the lake, where the canoes were moored. Soon the heat was suffocating, and she lay beside her two children, grateful they were sleeping and unaware of danger. She was parched with thirst, and she could hear the crack and roar of the flames, feel the heat on her face.

Only a miracle can save us, Susanna thought.

Outside, she could hear the wind blowing hard. Suddenly there was a great peal of thunder. The storm that had been gathering for several weeks finally broke, soaked the earth, and put out the fire in only a few minutes. The cabin and everyone in it was spared.

From then on, Susanna was haunted by a nightmare in which she saw herself carry her two children through flames, all their clothing catching fire. The fire in the fallow around the cabin and the recurring nightmare inspired her poem "The Forgotten Dream."

∞

In the summer of 1835, the Moodies made a memorable outing farther north into the Canadian wilderness to Stony Lake. Today a well-known resort, Stony Lake was then pristine, and a haven for First Nations people who tried to keep the colonists away by telling them frightening tales.

Early one morning, Susanna cuddled with Katie and Agnes in the canoe while John paddled several hours up Lake Katchewanooka to Young's Point. There, as arranged, they met their guide Mat Young, the son of the mill owner. Mat invited the Moodies to partake of a meal at his father's house before they travelled farther. The meal turned out to be a feast laid out on a wooden table daintily covered in a white linen cloth. *What abundance of food there is in Canada!* Susanna thought, as she marvelled at the roasts of venison, pork, chicken, duck, and several kinds of fish. She tasted the pickled cucumbers and the "green cheese" which turned out to be cream cheese. For dessert, she could choose from pumpkin, raspberry, cherry, and currant pies. She didn't like the coffee that was served, which had been boiled in a frying pan and had a vile taste.

The Moodies decided to entrust their two girls to the care of Mat's sisters and left in Mat's birchbark canoe. As he paddled them up Clear Lake, Mat entertained John with stories of his encounters with bears and wolves. Susanna preferred to lose herself in the beauty of the colourful wildflowers that grew profusely along the shores.

"I can show you a pretty spot where an Indian is buried," Mat offered. "He drowned during a storm off Sandy Point."

After securing the canoe, Susanna followed Mat through thick bushes. She smelled the rich odour of wild roses. They stopped at a mound of stones, which marked the gravesite. What moved Susanna were the tufts of blue harebells that peeked among the crevices.

"I haven't seen harebells since I left England," Susanna exclaimed. "They were my favourite flowers when I was a child."

She knelt and gathered a few sprigs. *How good it would be to walk the hills and commons of England again!* Susanna mused as she held the precious bouquet and breathed in the sweet scent.

She brought her scented treasure back with her to the canoe and showed it to John. He had rested and was ready to go on. When they finally arrived at Stony Lake, Susanna couldn't take in all the wild nature that she saw: the sun was setting and cast a golden light upon thousands of islands of different sizes, covered in huckleberry, cranberry, and raspberry bushes, and spread out on a bright sheet of emerald-tinted water. Overwhelmed by a love for what she would record later as "a landscape, savage and grand in its primeval beauty," Susanna no longer regretted her separation from her native country and began to feel at peace with Canada.

∞

In the winter of 1837, a second fire nearly made Susanna's recurring nightmare become reality.

Always in need of help, Susanna had hired a young Irish girl as a servant. On her second day, the girl, who wanted to be useful, had taken it upon herself to fill the Franklin stove in the parlour with cedar chips, which burned more rapidly than the green wood available. Within minutes, the cabin was filled with heavy smoke, and to Susanna's consternation, the roof caught fire. She sent the hysterical servant the mile through the woods to get help at the Traills' home.

Katie helped Susanna drag heavy furniture out of the house into the frigid cold. Soon John appeared, along with Thomas and Samuel, to douse the flames with countless pails of frozen snow.

Again, miraculously, there was little damage to the cabin, but from that day, Susanna nervously eyed the flames that crackled in the hearth of her unprotected bush home.

Each winter the situation at the Moodie farm worsened, rather than improved. Susanna, who in 1836 had borne a fourth child, Donald, was certain she and John had made a mistake to believe they could survive as pioneers in the bush. She had come to resent how the British government had, in her opinion, tricked gentlemen such as her husband into thinking they could better their lives with the offer of free land.

What seemed like a good idea on paper was proving to be tragic for many families of the Queen's Army. This bitter truth was embodied in the family of Captain

Frederick Lloyd in the village of Dummer. Susanna had come to hear of their plight through Jenny Buchanan, her servant.

Jenny had worked for the Lloyds for five years with little pay and often visited the children she'd helped to raise. She witnessed the deterioration of the captain, who had become a drunkard, unable to tolerate the isolation and hard work required of him in the bush. After mistreating his family, he had decided to join the rebel band of William Lyon Mackenzie in the United States.

Susanna, touched by Jenny's account of the destitution of the abandoned children, decided to go to Dummer with her friend Amelia and Thomas Traill to bring provisions. It was January, and the three of them had to trudge through knee-deep snow and cross many frozen creeks. Thomas decided to wait for the two women at a nearby cottage. When Susanna and Amelia entered the Lloyds' cabin, they were shocked to see Ella, the mother, dressed in a thin muslin gown, and her ragtag children barefoot and thin from starvation. Stubbornly, Ella said she didn't want their help, but the children begged her to accept it.

"We have sold our cow," one of the older boys explained, "but were swindled by the farmer who gave us notes from the Farmers' Bank that aren't valid. We've only eaten potatoes and no bread or meat for eighteen months."

"Ella," Susanna pleaded, "do accept these loaves that Jenny baked for you. And we have ham, fish, beef, tea, and sugar."

"I will make you a meal, then," Ella said.

Susanna and Amelia accepted, for they were hungry from their trip, but Thomas suddenly arrived and insisted they had to return home right away, as it was getting dark. When Susanna at last arrived back at the cabin, she had fasted for twelve hours and walked more than twelve kilometres on an iron-cold day. She had seen how destitute an abandoned woman with small children in the bush could be. Something similar was soon to be her own fate.

6

Letter to the Governor

When the day dawned, the whole forest scenery lay glittering in a mantle of dazzling white; the sun shone brightly, the heavens were intensely blue, but the cold was so severe that every article of food had to be thawed before we could get our breakfast. The very blankets that covered us during the night were stiff with our frozen breath. "I hope the sleighs won't come today," I cried; "we should be frozen on the long journey."
– Susanna Moodie, *Roughing It in the Bush*

In December 1837, the name William Lyon Mackenzie became familiar, and abhorrent, to

John Lovell, Montreal QC, 1865.
Photograph by William Notman (1828-1891).
The Montreal publisher John Lovell gave his financial support and
personal warmth to Susanna at a critical time in her writing life.

Susanna and John Moodie. Mackenzie was the fire-brand editor of the *Colonial Advocate* and a member of the Upper Canada legislature. He also led an insurrection against the British government. The Queen's Proclamation, a call for volunteers to join the Queen's Battalion to fight the rebels, was delivered one cold snowy evening at the Moodies' door, along with a letter from Catharine. Susanna read Catharine's letter aloud to John, who was resting near the fire.

The letter announced that Thomas had already gone ahead to Toronto, along with Samuel, but that Susanna had to persuade John not to go, since it would be too dangerous for him. He had broken a leg while at work in the field and had to use crutches. John would not listen to reason. It was his duty to go:

"Prepare my things," he ordered Susanna, his normally sweet voice sharp to her ears.

∞

William Lyon Mackenzie and his band of rebels were soon routed by the Queen's army. To Susanna's joy, John returned to her a few days later.

What would happen next? Even though Mackenzie was now in exile in the United States, the British colony had been traumatized. The government formed a new regiment named the Queen's Own, to defend the borders. John was appointed a captain with full pay for six months.

On January 20, 1838, John left the homestead again. Susanna's darkest period now began, as the "light of her life" as she referred to her husband, was gone. She was pregnant again. How could she survive a winter in the bush alone? The bright side to the desperate situation was that John sent her money to pay the debts incurred mostly for help at the farm. He even sent Susanna fabric for clothes for herself and the children, who at last had shoes to wear. And she could pay their servant Jenny Buchanan, who was as strong as any man and did everything cheerfully.

Clever Jenny had concocted a way for Susanna to be able to write at night, in the light of what she called "sluts," rags dipped in pork lard and stuck in a bottle. Yet Jenny didn't care at all for books:

"Shure we can live and die without them. Its only a waste of time botherin' your brains wid the like of them."

Susanna tried to concentrate but Jenny wouldn't stop talking:

"An' sure, you are killin' yerself that you are intirely. You were thin enough before you took to the pen, scribblin' and scrabblin' when you should be in bed asleep. What good will it be to the children, dear heart, if you die afore your time by wastin' your strength after that fashion?"

Susanna's British blood was boiling at Mackenzie's act of rebellion. Passionate poems to inspire others to rally round the British flag came from her pen, with titles such as "The Oath of the Canadian Volunteers" and "An Address to the Freemen of Canada":

Canadians! will you join the band –
The factious band – who dare oppose
The regal power of that bless'd land
From whence your boasted freedom flows?

Brave children of a noble race,
Guard well the altar and the hearth;
And never by your deeds disgrace
The British sires who gave you birth.

She sent these *Patriotic Songs* to John in Toronto, who passed them on to newspapers such as the *Palladium of British America*. Some poems were quickly reprinted in other newspapers. Susanna's name became a familiar one to the colonists of Upper Canada who responded to her passionate call. Even the lieutenant-governor, Sir George Arthur, read her words with admiration.

∞

Tears of joy streamed down Susanna's lined face as she clutched the crumpled twenty-dollar bill to her chest. She had earned this money from her pen. Wasn't it proof that her writing had worth? An editor in Montreal, John Lovell, wanted more of her work, and would pay for it. Lovell had emigrated from Scotland, and he appreciated Susanna's patriotic sentiments. He wanted her to be a regular contributor to his new magazine, the *Literary Garland*. The postage would be paid and she could name her own terms. Though Susanna didn't reap the benefits immediately, a new era in her life was beginning.

∞

Even pregnant, Susanna was unstoppable that first winter alone with Jenny and the children. And in May

1838, her brother-in-law Thomas proudly wrote to John, still in Toronto:

"Your wife deserves all you say of her. She has commanded the esteem of everyone. Your spring crops are nearly in… in fact she is farther advanced than her brother or me, or indeed any of the neighbors… I am happy to say that all your children look fat, fair and flourishing…"

This news surely reassured John, who was preparing to return to the bush, his post coming to an end. Susanna was troubled by the fact that John would no longer earn a salary. She couldn't imagine reliving the depth of poverty they had before. One sleepless night, filled with anguish, Susanna knelt on her bed, and prayed:

"God, direct me. Guide me. What should we do?"

Soon a peaceful feeling overcame her, and she lay down. Then, she distinctly heard these words: "Write to the Governor; tell him candidly all you have suffered during your sojourn in this country, and trust to God for the rest."

For a few minutes Susanna resisted the other-worldly suggestion, but soon she got out of bed and composed a letter addressed to Sir George Arthur, the lieutenant-governor of Upper Canada.

She explained all that they had suffered so far and what they needed: for John to stay in the militia at full pay, so that their debts could be paid. She sent the letter, although she knew she would have to keep it a secret from John, her first secret from him. He wouldn't approve of this missive, which was asking for a favour, but what other choice did they have?

∽

When John returned to the cabin in Douro at the beginning of August, he was just in time to help reap the harvest. These were weeks of peace and harmony and the couple dwelled only on the joy of being together. On October 16, 1838, Susanna gave birth to their fifth child, a healthy boy they named John Strickland and nicknamed Johnnie.

A few days later, John received an official letter. He had been appointed paymaster for the militia of Victoria District. Susanna guessed this was Sir George Arthur's response to her letter. John would be leaving again, this time for the town of Belleville, more than sixty kilometres away. Because John's position was temporary, Susanna would stay with the children, and the servant, Jenny, at the bush cabin. Susanna felt optimistic. Hadn't she coped well the previous winter?

∽

The Traills' log cabin was filled with the delicious smells of roast goose and plum pudding, and the fire crackled in the Franklin stove as Susanna helped Catharine clean the wood table of the remains of the Christmas feast.

The gifts from the Strickland family in England were unwrapped and strewn about the small room: beautiful children's books, bolts of fabric for clothing for everyone, silk stockings, and more of Agnes's discarded ball gowns. Their elder sister, still single, hobnobbed with the wealthy set, for her biographies of the royal family were best-sellers. Susanna listened to the excited cries of the children as they played in the snow with Thomas.

"I do wish Mother could see the children one day." Susanna said, as she wiped a platter with a cloth.

"Susie, we'll go back to England one day soon. We'll visit Reydon Hall and embrace our dearest. We just have to believe that," Catharine replied.

She turned from the sink and smiled, her pretty face flushed from the heat in the cabin. How happy Susanna felt just being near her sister: *What will I do if she moves away?* She was worried because Thomas, always so helpful, had now put the Traill farm up for sale. He no longer could manage the land or the piling up of debts.

∞

Twenty-four hours later, when Thomas had driven Susanna and the children back to their cabin in his sleigh, he noticed that Susanna looked feverish and in pain. Her left arm had swollen up, and she was unable to nurse baby Johnnie.

Too weak to raise herself up, Susanna lay on her bed. Jenny hovered around her and clucked her tongue in distress. "Och, Och the poor thing has a fever. Send for the doctor please."

"I will go for Dr. Hutchinson," Thomas said.

When Dr. Hutchinson arrived from Peterborough, seven kilometres away, he diagnosed mastitis, an infection of the breast that could be fatal. Quickly he lanced the abscess that was poisoning Susanna.

The wailing of the Moodie children aggravated the pathetic scene in the isolated cabin. Appalled at how dirty and drafty the place was, Dr. Hutchinson exclaimed before leaving:

"Mrs. Moodie, In the name of God, you must get out of this."

∽

More illness came, this time to the children. Two-year-old Donald severely cut his head on the corner of the iron stove, then fell ill with scarlet fever, an inflammation of the lungs with high fever. The baby also caught the disease. This time, Dr. Hutchinson couldn't come, for the roads were impassable with snow.

With Jenny's help, Susanna tended to the children and didn't take time to sleep. The children survived, but Susanna collapsed with influenza.

Neighbours rallied to help. Mary Hague, a wealthy friend from Peterborough, took five-year-old Agnes into her house, and four-year-old Dunbar went to another family. Food was left on the cabin's doorstep: duck or venison, gifts from the Chippewa. Susanna was overwhelmed by this generosity and thought, *You must become poor yourself before you can fully appreciate the good qualities of the poor – before you can sympathize fully with them, and fully recognize them as your brethren in the flesh.*

If she had stayed in England, Susanna now asked herself, would she have experienced such destitution? Ironically, she and John had come to Canada to escape poverty, not knowing how much more they would suffer.

She felt she had sought a better world and now, like the Pilgrim, was in the Valley of the Shadow of Death.

∞

In that period of separation, Susanna and John exchanged letters, thin sheets of paper criss-crossed with news and passionate declarations of love. Susanna believed in what she called the "communion of spirits," a mystical bonding she experienced with her loved ones. She noticed that John often wrote to her on the very day and hour she had been thinking of him most. Susanna needed to hear from John regularly, or else she would lose her courage. She no longer had Catharine and Thomas to count on, for they had sold their farm and moved seven kilometres away to the village of Ashburnham, near Peterborough.

On July 16, 1839, Susanna could no longer hide her desperation from John and wrote in a letter:

"Such another winter as the last will pile the turf over my head. I cannot help crying when I think, that such, may be in store for me. While I had you to comfort and support me all trials seemed light, but left to myself, in this solitude, with only old Jenny to speak to, and hearing so seldom of you makes my life a burden to me."

Susanna no longer cared for the farm. As a pioneer, she wanted to give up. But as a writer, she continued to struggle, and what gave her hope was her connection with the *Literary Garland* and its publisher John Lovell, who paid her for every poem and article she sent.

Good news at last came in a letter from Moodie: he had been appointed sheriff of Victoria District, a permanent post. He could now look for a house in Belleville for Susanna and the children.

∞

A few days after Christmas 1839, when the snow stopped falling, two sleighs arrived at the Moodies' cabin. Susanna was ready. Over the last months, she had been busier than ever. She had secured someone to take over the farm and had sold the farm equipment and the live-stock. She had even sewn a new gown for herself from the fabric John sent from Belleville after she wrote to him of her fear that she was "no longer fit for the world."

The hardscrabble living in the bush for seven years had changed Susanna in many ways. Her fair British skin had wrinkled and her figure had coarsened from the harsh climate and the onerous chores. She had turned thirty-seven years old, and she felt every bit her age as Jenny helped her load up the sleighs with the few belongings left to take.

To her great relief, Samuel unexpectedly arrived in his large comfortable sleigh to take Susanna and the children to Belleville. She needed her brother's take-charge presence. As the time to leave grew close, Susanna sat in the sleigh and relaxed. She had said farewell to her friends, the Chippewa neighbours. Katie, Dunbar, Donald, and Johnnie, were curled up in the furs beside her on the bench. Soon she would be reunited with her daughter Agnes in Peterborough. Only Jenny was missing.

At last the servant appeared at the doorway of the cabin. Susanna and Samuel and all the children laughed out loud at what they saw. Jenny had piled the four hats she owned one on top of the other onto her head: a sky-blue silk bonnet, a dirty yellow calico hat, a battered straw hat with pink ribbons, and a grey beaver bonnet, gift from Susanna.

"Go back, Jenny," Samuel ordered. "For God's sake take all that tomfoolery from off your head. We shall be the laughingstock of every village we pass through."

Jenny wasn't pleased with his reaction: "Och, shure now, Mr. Strickland, who'd think of looking at an old crathur like me! Its only yersel' that would notice the like."

"All the world, " Samuel said with a smile, "would look at you, Jenny. I believe that you put on those hats to draw the attention of all the young fellows that we shall happen to meet on the road!"

Jenny climbed into the sleigh after she had finally removed the hats. She held them tightly on her lap. Samuel clicked his tongue and the horses began to move down the forest path. In the dimming light, Susanna's chest tightened with apprehension, and she kept looking back at the log cabin and the lake until she couldn't see them anymore. She was travelling again to an unknown destination, a new life. Would it prove to be a better one? Would she now have more time to write and publish?

The cold was so severe they had to stop several times at strangers' farms to warm up the children. They picked up six-year-old Agnes at the home of Mary Hague in Peterborough. Agnes, who had lived there for several months, began to cry and cling to Mary. Susanna thanked her friend for her devoted care of her "noisy little pet," and soon managed to convince Agnes to climb into the sleigh and join the other children.

In Belleville, John anxiously awaited his family in their comfortable new home, a modest cottage. He had even purchased a new china tea service for Susanna, so she could serve four o'clock tea once again.

The politician Robert Baldwin, now known as
the "Father of Responsible Government,"
became a close friend to the Moodies in Belleville.
In 1843, they named their fourth son after him.

7

Colonial Woes

> A new country, where all are rushing eagerly
> forward in order to secure the common nec-
> essaries of life, is not a favourable soil in
> which to nourish the bright fancies and
> delusive dreams of the poet.
> – Susanna Moodie, *Life in the Clearings*

As sheriff of Victoria District, in which Belleville was the largest town, John quickly made enemies. His promotion had come through Sir George Arthur. Canadian-born men were irked that a British emigrant had been preferred over themselves. Thomas Parker, a postmaster who had expected to receive the appointment, resigned in protest.

In 1840, colonial towns were still reacting to William Lyon Mackenzie's rebel cry against the British government and had divided citizens into two distinct factions: Tories and Reformers. As a Reformer, John was suspect due to his loyalty to Queen Victoria, and so was Susanna when she arrived in Belleville, cold and sick from the rough journey out of the bush.

Belleville women were as fiercely political as their husbands, and friendships were determined not by any psychic affinity, as Susanna would have it, but by political affiliation. Her hope of meeting other women who could share her literary aspirations was soon crushed. Susanna proudly used her new china tea service when neighbours paid her a visit, but none of the visitors came back, and she soon learned why: she was a disappointment. She was a published author but she didn't look any different from anyone else.

"What did they expect?" Susanna asked John.

"Someone who would stand on her head," he joked.

The cottage John had purchased fit the needs of Susanna and the ever growing family. The Moodies were expecting their sixth child, due in July. Susanna didn't like the town, which she saw upon arrival as an "insignificant, dirty-looking place." Belleville had nothing of the architectural charm of what she remembered of Bungay, or Southwold. There wasn't a market, and most of the small houses were wood frame, painted an ugly yellow or green. On Front Street, where a few brick buildings served as stores, Susanna often tripped and damaged her shoes against the badly laid-out slabs of stones.

She was grateful to be able to attend church again, but she didn't think much of St. Thomas Anglican Church, which she described as an "eyesore."

What Susanna did admire was the beauty of the rural landscape, the hills and woods that surrounded the town. Always sensitive to the presence of water, Susanna rejoiced at Belleville's location on the Bay of Quinte. She took walks along the Moira River and enjoyed the silvery waters that ran parallel with the main street. The Moira was a rapid and picturesque stream with rocky banks of limestone fringed with cedars, maples, and rock elms.

In the spring, Susanna was amused by the French-Canadian loggers. She thought they looked as lithe and active as wildcats as they jumped from log to log, making their way down the river with their long poles.

∞

The baby was born in the heat of July and was named George Arthur to honour the man who had helped the Moodies change their life for the better. But within three weeks, the baby died.

Susanna was still recovering from her loss when, a few months later, a fire broke out in the cottage. The flames spread quickly through the rooms, the wooden furniture fuel for the fire. There was little time to escape.

Susanna gathered all the children and rushed them outside. John stayed behind to look for two-year-old Johnnie. The November wind rushed through the open windows to fan the flames while Susanna prayed that John could find their boy in time. The flames had reached the roof when John came out with Johnnie in his arms.

"He'd crawled under a table in the kitchen," Moodie told her as she held out her arms to the baby. "It was dark and I couldn't see him. Then I heard him cry, thank God."

The fire took most of their belongings, including their clothes and provisions for the winter months, but no one had been hurt. Susanna could cope because she had John by her side, the marital knot growing stronger through these trials.

Soon after, the Moodies relocated to a stately stone house on Bridge Street, along the Moira River. Though not situated in the best part of Belleville, the house, which would be their home for twenty years, was attractive and spacious, with a front verandah, and a separate wing at the rear for the kitchen. Susanna had a maid to help her with the children and a handyman to do the work around the house. She also had a writing table, where she worked for hours with little interruption. John Lovell's *Literary Garland* published the manuscripts she submitted, and Susanna made all the money she needed to pay for postage, paper, and family necessities. Her reputation as a writer in Canada was established: her name was as well known as other colonial authors of the time, Rosa Leprohon and Charles Sangster.

～

Susanna wrote letters to her mother and Agnes to tell them about her literary successes. She described a trip to Montreal to meet her publisher, John Lovell, and his wife. She had made a special purchase there – a piano.

On a cold day in late November, the family gathered in the parlour, the children peeking out the window every few minutes, though no one was sure when the longed-for piano would at last arrive. Owning a piano was the status symbol of the day, but the reason Susanna wanted one was not just to impress Belleville's burghers, but for her girls.

Suddenly the children cried out: "It's here, it's here!"

Susanna rushed to open the door as the burly men brought in the blanketed and roped piano from the cart outside.

The piano was perfect. Susanna was especially pleased when her pretty Agnes sat at the bench and fingered the keys with interest. She wanted both Agnes and Katie to learn to play the piano, which she felt would add polish to their beauty. Answering the family's pleas, Susanna sat down and played a few short pieces to warm up, and then they all sang favourite hymns.

What added to Susanna's joy was that she was paying for the piano with her earnings from the *Literary Garland*.

～

On July 8, 1843, Susanna gave birth to another boy. He was healthy and sweet tempered, and the proud parents chose to name him Robert Baldwin after their newest friend, the rising politician and leader of the Reform Party of the United Provinces. Baldwin lived in Belleville at that time and often visited the Moodies at their home. They had grown close to the thirty-six-year-old lawyer from Toronto, who was a widower with four children.

When Baldwin was the Moodies' guest, the conversation was always lively with ideas and dreams. They all agreed that a better education system was needed in the colony. Children did not have a high level of education and something had to be done. Robert Baldwin was the man who, given the power, would change the standards in the growing colony. His vision that Canada would grow to be a great nation stimulated the hopes of the Moodies.

Baldwin admired Susanna's writings and shared his own poems about the loss of his wife Eliza, more than five years earlier. He couldn't overcome his grief and was haunted by how she had died in childbirth. This sensitive, cultured, Irish Canadian was a worthy namesake for their newest child.

∽

One afternoon in the spring of 1844, Susanna was busy in the kitchen making bread, a task she had become so skilful at that she had won a prize at the local fair. She was trying to shake off a dream she'd had the night before, which was still troubling her. She had been in

Reydon Hall again, filled with excitement as she held little Johnnie's hand:

"You will meet your grandmother today," she had told her favourite child.

As always, Johnnie's bright smile had made her heart fill with pride. Her mother would see with her own eyes how well Susanna had done in Canada, what a special grandchild she had.

Then her older sister Jane had materialized, grim-faced as ever:

"Mother is dead, Susanna."

"Dead?" Susanna had repeated. "Dead?"

Jane continued coldly:

"Yes. She died a long time ago but we didn't want to tell you. You already have enough sorrows to bear."

As she mixed the flour and water for the bread, Susanna still felt burdened, as if her mother really had died, though she knew it couldn't be true. Only the week before, Agnes had sent her a letter telling her how well their mother was keeping.

"Mother, Johnnie is missing!"

Donald's shout as he ran into the kitchen frightened Susanna. Her hands still white with flour, she rushed into the living room where John was reading.

"Please go to the river," Susanna cried out. "Something's happened to Johnnie."

John rushed out, with eight-year-old Donald leading the way. To keep busy while she waited, Susanna continued with her bread making. She now sensed her dream had been a warning. Within an hour, John returned, holding in his arms the limp wet body of her dear Johnnie. The six-year-old boy had fallen off the dock and drowned in the Moira River.

A few months later, heartbroken, Susanna would begin her poem, "A Mother's Lament," with these mournful lines:

Oh, cold at my feet thou wert sleeping, my boy,
And I press on thy pale lips in vain the fond kiss!
Earth opens her arms to receive thee, my joy,
And all my past sorrows were nothing to this.

Susanna walked quickly along Front Street towards the Victoria Bookstore, where she had business to take care of. She marvelled at how Belleville had grown since she had first arrived seven years earlier. The Bay of Quinte was busy with vessels, and she counted many more stone wharves. Buildings and shops had multiplied, and the women she passed wore fashionable dresses. At the storefront that advertised: *The Belleville Intelligencer – George Benjamin, Proprietor*, Susanna's elated mood changed to disgust. The Tory editor was John's worst enemy. He used his newspaper to slander Moodie's name and that of their friend Robert Baldwin.

Susanna used her own pen to get back at Benjamin. She created a despicable character based on the *Belleville Intelligencer* editor and named him Benjamin Levi in her story, "Richard Redpath: A Tale." She had the satisfaction of seeing it in print, not only in the *Literary Garland*, but also in the *Toronto Star*.

Susanna hurried on, taking deep breaths of fresh air, anxious to escape the possibility of running into

Benjamin. She was on her way to meet a friendlier man, the publisher Joseph Wilson, at his bookstore. He had invited her and John to co-edit the *Victoria Magazine*. Wasn't this the literary opportunity she had hoped for when she had first arrived in the colony?

∞

Susanna and John put their heads together and made the monthly *Victoria Magazine* an "excellent journal" that was praised in the newspapers. Susanna wanted to encourage local talent and published a romantic tale by one of her younger admirers, Louisa Murray of Kingston, Ontario.

She had relished announcing to her famous sister Agnes in England that she was the editor of a magazine. To Susanna's surprise, Agnes, who was working on her ninth volume on British royalty, graciously sent her a lengthy article entitled "The Death of Edward, Prince of Wales."

Susanna was now passionate about something too, though it didn't exude any whiff of royalty. Her favourite subject was her own experience as a pioneer in the bush. She had written "Canadian Sketches" with such plain titles as "A Visit to Grosse Isle" and "First Impressions, Quebec." They appeared in the *Victoria Magazine* and in the *Literary Garland*. She had kept all her writings about the bush ordeal, and John encouraged her to use them for a book. Why not? Hadn't Catharine published her early letters to England in *The Backwoods of Canada*?

My book, Susanna reflected, *will have a completely different point of view from Catharine's: it will be a warning to the British people who want to become pioneers, not a cheerful book at all.*

8

Fame and Family Rejection

An English lady, writing to me not long ago,
expressed her weariness of my long story
about the country of my adoption, in the following terms – "Don't fill your letters to me
with descriptions of Canada. Who, in
England, thinks anything of Canada!"
— Susanna Moodie, *Life in the Clearings*

In the privacy of the second-floor bedroom, Susanna
reread the letter she had just received from Agnes,
an angry letter that sickened Susanna. She would have
torn it into bits then and there, but she wanted John to
read it too as soon as he returned from his appointment in town. She guessed John would be as shocked

Agnes Strickland in England was famous for her biographies of royalty. Susanna sorely regretted having dedicated her first book to her elder sister, who judged it "vulgar" and ceased corresponding with Susanna.

as she was at her elder sister's outrageous demand that Susanna remove the dedication from her newly published book, *Roughing It in the Bush*.

It simply read:

To Agnes Strickland
Author of the "Lives of the Queens of England"
This simple Tribute of Affection
is dedicated
by her sister
Susanna Moodie

How can Agnes be so mean-spirited! Is she embarrassed by my dedication? Susanna pondered. Her elder sister complained in her letter at what she deemed the vulgarity of the people and scenes in the book. And Agnes boasted that she was a guest at Kensington Palace, that she mingled among the "Lords and Ladies," and wore a tiara at the balls she attended.

The light was dimming. Susanna got up from the bed to light a candle. How could Agnes rant that she should never have published *Roughing It in the Bush*, not even for money? "You should have burnt the whole manuscript," she wrote.

Susanna's delicate stomach ached from the blow. She heard John's footsteps on the staircase. He was coming to her rescue again, though he didn't know it yet.

"Susie," he called to her as he entered their bedroom: "Katie is preparing supper. She says you are unwell."

"Read this, John, from Agnes."

Gently, John sat beside her and took the letter from her hand.

Susanna gazed at her husband's careworn face, softened by the thick fleece of white hair, and waited for him to speak.

"My dear," John said, as he folded the letter back up, "Agnes has completely misunderstood you and your worthy book."

These words of sympathy were a balm to Susanna. She lay her head on her husband's frail shoulder, felt his arm around her waist. However difficult their life had been since they had married and emigrated to Canada, Susanna felt no regrets. They were meant for each other. Who did Agnes have to love? She was just a bitter old maid, that was all.

A year later in 1853, when a second edition was printed, Susanna wrote in a calmer mood to her publisher in London, Richard Bentley:

"I am really glad, that you have withdrawn the dedication to my sister... She has wounded my feelings so severely about this dedication that it is a perfect eye sore in front of my unfortunate book. Could I have foreseen her reception of it, thousands would not have induced me to place it there."

∞

To Susanna's satisfaction, brisk sales of *Roughing It in the Bush* were bringing her much-needed money. Dunbar, now a fit sixteen-year-old, wanted to go to California. Pleased that her eldest son showed some ambition, Susanna paid for his trip. Her daughter Agnes had needed monetary help since she had married Charles Thomas Fitzgibbon, a Toronto lawyer who gambled. Susanna's earnings never stretched far enough, and things didn't improve when a pirated edition of *Roughing It in the Bush* was sold in the United States. Susanna didn't receive any royalties, even though *Roughing It* rivalled Harriet Beecher Stowe's *Uncle Tom's Cabin* as a bestseller of the day.

President Abraham Lincoln once remarked upon meeting Harriet Beecher Stowe that the five-foot author was "the little lady who started the big war." Susanna was more like the tall lady who started the battle in her own backyard. *Roughing It in the Bush* exposed the dark side of emigration and the mental and physical bondage a pioneer experienced in the backwoods. Some reviewers didn't like this and accused her of debasing Canada. Others wrote that she slighted the Irish in her book. Susanna felt misunderstood: she had written nothing but the truth.

∞

"Agnes tells me my book is on every table in London," Samuel declared to Susanna and John at their dining table, as he cut into another piece of roast chicken.

"Is that so?" Susanna responded, somewhat sarcastically. She knew better. Sam's memoir *Twenty-Seven Years in Canada West*, had been praised in the English press but wasn't selling, according to Bentley, who had published her younger brother's book. As Samuel regaled John with another one of his backwoods hunting anecdotes, Susanna ate, her stomach in a knot – as it usually was when she held her tongue. She looked at Samuel, now heavyset, a wealthy landowner and newly widowed. She would like to tell him his memoir was "pompous and boring" and that the language was false because rough Canadians didn't speak as if they were in an English drawing-room. Samuel's memoir had been Agnes's idea. Her name had even appeared on the title page: Agnes Strickland, Editor.

Susanna also knew Agnes had been the one to approach Richard Bentley, Susanna's own editor, but she didn't feel resentment toward him for printing the memoir, for she understood business. Bentley had agreed to publish *Mark Hurdlestone*, her novel written in the bush cabin in Douro. What she did resent was how Samuel was oblivious to her work. He only talked about his. She was glad that Samuel was leaving in the morning.

"Why does it say 'Major Strickland' on the title page?" Susanna asked. "I never heard you use this title before."

Across from her at the dining table, Samuel turned red as the cranberry sauce that accompanied the roasted fowl.

"Agnes thought it a good idea. She puts a lot of weight on titles, as you know. "

"Yes, Sam, I know. Should I call you Major, then?"

She was teasing him, but Samuel ignored the question. He had his appetite to satisfy and cut into the meat for another mouthful. John winked at Susanna. He understood how she needed to express her distaste for her brother's insensitivity.

∞

When Susanna wanted news from Reydon Hall, she was dependent on Catharine, for no one wrote to her anymore, not even her eighty-year-old mother, who was confined to her bedroom. Since her debacle with Agnes over the dedication to *Roughing It in the Bush*, Susanna had been cut off from the family.

She needed Catharine and invited her to Belleville often. Catharine enjoyed the town as she was now living in an isolated farmhouse on Rice Lake, far north of Peterborough. In 1852, Catharine published a children's book, *Canadian Crusoes*, which was well reviewed and highly approved of by the Strickland family, unlike Susanna's book. The lump sum Catharine received was quickly spent on necessities, because Thomas Traill was in a constant state of depression and couldn't work. When Susanna invited her sister to visit, Thomas stayed behind in the care of his capable elder daughters, Katie and Annie. The youngest daughter, Mary, lived with the Moodies for months at a time to attend school in Belleville. Catharine was grateful for Susanna's help, but she didn't take sides in the conflict between her and Agnes. Susanna resented this neutrality but understood how Catharine needed Agnes's gifts of money and clothing.

∞

The two sisters were in the Victoria Bookstore to browse the many shelves of leather-bound books. Susanna asked Catharine what the latest news was from England. She always feared hearing that their mother had taken ill, or even died.

"Mother is doing well enough," Catharine reassured her while admiring a volume of Canadian flora and fauna, her passion. She was thinking of all she had to write down for her newest book, a kind of settler's guide, with tips on how to grow and use medicinal plants, recipes for making bread, candles, pumpkin pie. Samuel had even promised her pages with instructions on how to build a log cabin. Susanna stared at her attractive blond, blue-eyed sister. They were so different, yet Susanna loved her sister as she had as a child, even when she had known Catharine was her father's favourite. Catharine was not a malicious person and certainly her sister's life in Canada had been as difficult as her own.

Back at Susanna's house for four o'clock tea, now served regularly to her family, Susanna asked Catharine if Agnes had sent her any parcels lately.

"Yes, I received one a week ago," Catharine answered. "There were some boots for the children that were useful."

She didn't mention that Agnes had also included in the same box a pair of long white gloves for her and cravats for the boys, which showed how little she understood of their meagre lifestyle. This information would irritate Susanna, and Catharine wanted to avoid this, for she felt her closest sister had suffered enough.

9

Niagara Falls

Yes, the great object of my journey – one of
the fondest anticipations of my life – was at
length accomplished; and for a moment the
blood recoiled back to my heart, and a
tremulous thrill ran through my whole
frame. I was so bewildered – so taken by
surprise – that every feeling was absorbed in
the one consciousness, that the sublime
vision was before me; that I had at last seen
Niagara...

    – Susanna Moodie, *Life in the Clearings*

In the fall of 1852, when Susanna was forty-eight, she
nearly died after several hemorrhages, probably

Susanna and John Moodie in Belleville. Their many trials
and sorrows had only strengthened their marriage.
Family members surround them.

from a stomach ulcer. Her "clever surgeons," as she referred to them in a letter to Richard Bentley, couldn't do any more for her and suggested a change of air. Susanna immediately knew where she would like to go. Her dream even as a child in England had been to see Niagara Falls. Since the late 1820s, Niagara had become a kind of pilgrimage site for tourists, as travellers had begun to be called. Charles Dickens, Susanna's favourite contemporary author, had published his extraordinary account of viewing the falls for the first time, and reading this had only increased Susanna's desire to see Niagara Falls for herself.

The Moodies were in a rare period of affluence. John, grateful to be able to do something for Susanna, made all the arrangements so that they travelled as comfortably as any Upper Canadian family of the day.

On a rainy morning, they boarded the steamboat *Chief Justice* on Lake Ontario. Susanna, depleted, hoped she might find at Niagara not only healing but also new material to write for Richard Bentley, who was pressing her hard for a sequel to *Roughing It in the Bush*. Because of the negative reviews and her family's rejection, Susanna had grown weary of the subject of Canada, but she might be inspired by this trip.

Autumn sunshine and a warm breeze had replaced the rain when the Moodies arrived in Queenston, where they climbed into the carriage bound for their destination. Susanna's first glimpse of the gushing waters from the window overwhelmed her frail mind and her intense emotional reaction was painful. *The falls are a sublime idea of the Eternal, a masterpiece of nature*, she thought.

The steamboat *The Maid of the Mist* brought the Moodies to Horseshoe Falls. From the little boat, Susanna sensed her helplessness and insignificance. She later wrote of this mystic experience:

The falls… flow down upon your vision like moving mountains of light; and the shadowy outline of black mysterious rocks, dimly seen through clouds of driving mist, adds a wild sublimity to the scene. While the boat struggles over the curling billows, at times lifted up by the groundswells from below, the feeling of danger and insecurity is lost in the whirl of waters that surround you. The mind expands with the scene, and you rejoice in the terrific power that threatens to annihilate you in your fairy bark. A visible presence of the majesty of God is before you, and, sheltered by His protecting hand, you behold the glorious spectacle and live.

∞

Several hours later, Susanna was sitting beside John at a table in the "eating-room" of the Clifton House. Only the moneyed could afford the elegant resort. Their room, like the best in the hotel, had French windows that opened onto a private balcony with a view onto the falls. The eating-room was half empty except for a party of Americans at a nearby table. Susanna was very hungry, but as she read the bill of fare she noticed the dishes had French names. How was she going to order? She heard an American express his displeasure in a loud voice:

"I hate these newfangled ways. I don't understand the French names for these dishes. I'm not French and it would be better if they were written in plain English."

Susanna exchanged a glance with John: at least she didn't divulge her ignorance to everyone as this man did. Dishes had been served at other tables and Susanna decided to point at the most appealing one for their waiter, a well-dressed black man, one of twelve who attended to the diners.

"These waiters are so quick and polite, aren't they, John?" Susanna observed, adding, in reference to the author of *Uncle Tom's Cabin*, "I am sure it would do Mrs. Stowe's heart good to see them for they must all be runaway slaves."

John agreed but didn't have time to reply, for the owner of the hotel had made his way to their table:

"Welcome to our establishment, Mr. and Mrs. Moodie. It is quite an honour to have such a famous lady among us. We hope everything is to your liking."

Susanna, warmed by the compliment, answered:

"Sir, we are particularly impressed by your fine corps of waiters."

"Yes, m'am," the owner replied. "I'm glad you noticed, for these Negroes far surpass any white men, in the neat elegant manner in which they lay out a table. I don't know what I would do without them."

After a few more minutes of pleasantries, the owner moved on to the table where the American guest continued to complain about the French bill of fare.

"Are you sure you want to step out again?" John inquired of Susanna as they finished their dessert.

Susanna had proposed a visit to the newly built Suspension Bridge, a mechanical wonder at seventy metres above the Niagara River. She was sure the bridge would be a worthy subject to write about.

The late outing turned out to be a disaster. The driver of the carriage was drunk and John had to sit by the window to block the view of the sharp cliffs from Susanna, who felt dizzy. Then, once on the Suspension Bridge, Susanna fainted.

Safely back in bed in the hotel room, Susanna couldn't sleep as she remembered all that she had seen so far. In awe of the natural beauty of the Niagara Peninsula, she felt upset that industry and commerce were blighting its shores. And human greed seemed bottomless. She'd heard the Americans were proposing to harness the hydraulic power of the falls to work machinery! In 1853, she published her concerns in a chapter of her new book *Life in the Clearings versus the Bush*:

"Niagara belongs to no particular nation or people... I trust that these free glad waters will assert their own rights, and dash into mist and spray any attempt to infringe their glorious liberty."

Susanna became a pioneer in a new way, as an early Canadian voice speaking out for the preservation of the environment.

∽

After Niagara Falls, the Moodies travelled to Toronto to visit their nineteen-year-old daughter Agnes, and her husband, Charles Fitzgibbon, the son of Colonel James

Fitzgibbon, a hero of the War of 1812 and the Rebellion of 1837. The Moodies were now grandparents, as Agnes had borne her first child, Mary.

In search of more subjects to write about, Susanna went with Agnes to the Toronto Lunatic Asylum, which was a tourist attraction at that time. Unlike her sister Catharine, who was fascinated by the study of nature, Susanna was attracted by the study of human nature. By focusing on the people around her, the more colourful or extreme the better, Susanna had learned to distract herself from her own anxieties and problems.

The Lunatic Asylum was a building of white brick, on spacious grounds with well-tended orchards and vegetable gardens. Susanna and Agnes joined a group who were being escorted through the different wards. An inmate suddenly rushed up and embraced Susanna, who held back, a little fearful:

"That's Mrs. Moodie, of Belleville. Many a good quarter I've got from her."

Susanna recognized the inmate as a Belleville neighbour whom she'd bought milk from.

"And this must be Agnes, your daughter. She's grown to be a fine beautiful girl, hasn't she?" the madwoman exclaimed with a wide grin. She then asked plaintively: "Do you know anything about my grown children?"

Susanna pretended she didn't, for the news was tragic. How could she add to this woman's desperate situation? She couldn't tell her that her young daughter had died, and her twenty-year-old son had, only months ago, flung himself off the bridge into the Moira River.

The ward keeper signalled for Susanna and Agnes to move on with the rest of the group. At the last ward they visited, they were allowed only to look at the inmates through a glass door for security reasons. Susanna felt more distressed than she expected at the sight of the "poor maniacs," whom she believed suffered "from a direful malady which certainly comes nearest to any form of demoniacal possession." Some danced grotesquely, others ran at full speed, laughed and shouted, their hands wrapped in cloth "mufflers," to prevent them from harming each other. Susanna recognized Grace Marks, a young woman who had been convicted of taking part in the gruesome murder of her employer, Thomas Kinnear, and his housekeeper, Nancy Montgomery.

After reading about the sensational trial in the newspapers, Susanna had been curious to see the infamous woman for herself. On a memorable day in 1849, she had accompanied John on his sheriff business to the Kingston Penitentiary. She'd asked the matron of the prison if she could meet Grace Marks. The matron obliged and called the young woman with long auburn hair to do some menial cleaning in the room. Susanna observed that Grace Marks was attractive except for a facial defect, a long, curved chin that gave her a "cunning look." The young prisoner, who had repented publicly of her crime, wouldn't speak or even look at Susanna and kept her gaze on the ground as she cleaned.

In the asylum, Grace Marks now fled, shrieking, into another room when she saw Susanna and the group of people staring through the glass. She returned to dance around a woman who was having a fit of rage. Susanna hurried away, repulsed at what she had just witnessed – the madwomen did not weep or lament their fate. Instead they laughed.

I fervently thank God for my sanity, Susanna thought as she left the asylum with Agnes.

∞

When Susanna returned home to Belleville, she still looked skeletal but she was strong enough to sit down at her writing desk again. Stimulated by her travel experiences, she was determined to write the sequel to *Roughing It in the Bush* that Richard Bentley was pleading for. Bentley had become a close friend she confided in. Susanna scanned the library shelves that held the treasured books he had sent her as gifts from London: poetry by Lord Tennyson and Henry Wadsworth Longfellow; essays by Ralph Waldo Emerson and Margaret Fuller; history books by William Doran; and novels by Thackeray and Dickens.

Susanna had several of her own novels she wanted to polish up for publication, but first she would finish this sequel about Canada. She decided to use the trip to Niagara Falls as the frame. For her British readers, who wouldn't know the tragic story, she wanted to include a chapter about Grace Marks. She would pad the book with chapters she had left out of *Roughing It*, including one about the death of the Irish boy, Michael Macbride. She'd cobble together genres: poems, travelogue, essay.

Susanna passionately wanted to defend novel writing. She began to write down how there were too many good and conscientious people who regarded novelists with devout horror and condemned their works as unfit. They believed that all works of fiction had a demoralizing effect, and weakened and enervated the mind.

Susanna reflected for a moment on her own favourite novel, *Oliver Twist*, considered controversial because of its vivid depiction of brutality and poverty in London. She wrote that this work by Charles Dickens had brought to light the oppressive circumstances suffered by the destitute, and many "thinking and benevolent persons," were "called upon to assist in the liberation of these *white slaves*, chained to the oar of life in the galleys of wealth, and to recognize them as men and brethren."

Within a few weeks, Bentley accepted the manuscript of *Life in the Clearings versus the Bush* and rushed it into print. The sales proved slow, and Susanna was disappointed, but Bentley promised to publish her novel *Mark Hurdlestone*, which had been serialized in the *Literary Garland*. Susanna was certain the sensationalistic tale about a man so obsessed with acquiring gold that he eventually goes mad from his crimes would sell, but again, she was disappointed.

These setbacks were taking a toll on Susanna's creativity. By the end of 1853, she felt so discouraged that she nearly came to the decision never to write again, and left her newest novel *Geoffrey Moncton* unfinished. But she confided to Bentley that her writing income was desperately needed by the family, for John's conflicts with the Tories of Belleville had escalated and he couldn't collect hundreds of dollars that were due him.

Bentley accepted Susanna's autobiographical novel, *Flora Lyndsay: or Passages in an Eventful Life*, for publication, but the story of her emigration to Canada didn't sell either. None of Susanna's other books matched the success of *Roughing It*.

Often, now, Susanna had acute pain in her hand and couldn't even pick up her pen. On December 12, 1858, she made the effort to answer a letter from Catharine and sadly confided how she could no longer come to the aid of her daughter: "Poor Aggie is penniless and I have not the means to help her, even with clothes of my own, for I am literally in rags – a misfortune which has seldom happened to me before."

Painting by Susanna Moodie: *"Goldfinch and Thistle."*
Susanna had talent as an artist, and in her later years
she often sold her paintings of nature for much-needed income.

10

Under a Spell

Earth is the vista through which Heaven is
seen...

– Susanna Moodie, *Enthusiasm
and Other Poems*

To the Moodies, money was never everything; they
had spiritual concerns. The American Civil War
had begun and there was little market for literature
from Canada as few people had time to read or money
to buy books. In the early 1860s, Susanna was, at first,
appalled that John had joined the popular Spiritualist
movement. He grew a lush beard, which made him
look like the controversial American poet Walt

Whitman on their copy of *Leaves of Grass*. And John published an anti-slavery poem in the Christian Guardian and articles in the *New York Spiritual Telegraph*.

Susanna didn't like the fact that John took so much time with the contraption he had invented and named a Spiritoscope nor the fact that he wrote incessantly of his mystical experiences in a blue leather-bound album he carried with him wherever he went.

Despite their differences, Susanna felt as close to her husband as on the day they had married, twenty-five years earlier. John was away on a business trip on their anniversary, and she received a gift by the post. She admired the beautiful gold locket that opened to reveal a picture of her husband, "You would laugh to see me regarding that white bearded face with the devotion of old times," she wrote to Catharine. "The old romance of my nature is not quite dead. The poetry of life still lingers about my heart."

John travelled to New York to consult with the Fox sisters, who were known among thousands of followers as the "Spirit Rappers" as they apparently could communicate with the dead. When John learned the sisters were born in Belleville and often visited relatives, he invited them to the Moodie house.

One autumn morning, the maid announced that Miss Kate Fox was at the door. John was on an errand, and Susanna, who was skeptical on the subject of Spiritualism but had just read and been captivated by the best-seller of the day, *The Healing of Nations*, stood alone with the famous medium in the drawing room. Now a matronly woman of fifty-two, Susanna gazed at the small figure of twenty-year-old Kate Fox and marvelled at her manners and her "magnetic" violet eyes, the "most beautiful eyes I'd ever seen in a human head."

Kate Fox no doubt wanted to impress the well-known Canadian author and make her a convert to the Spiritualist movement.

"Please lay your hand on the table, Mrs. Moodie," she requested.

Susanna did as she was told. She thought she felt the table vibrate under her palm, as if endowed with life.

"Stand by the door, Mrs. Moodie." When Fox placed a hand on her shoulder, the door shook and vibrated.

Out in the garden, Susanna stood on a rock and felt hollow raps under her feet.

"Are you still unbelieving?" Fox inquired.

"I think these knocks are made by your spirit, not by the dead," Susanna replied.

Fox assured her:

"You attribute more power to me than I possess. Would you believe if you heard that piano, closed as it is, play a tune?"

For this event, Susanna invited Fox to return the next evening when John would be home. As he played a melody on the flute, while Fox stood by the piano, they were amazed to hear the strings accompany him, the lid firmly shut. *Is this pretty dark-haired young woman a witch?* Susanna wondered.

Since she'd left the Anglican Church in her early twenties, Susanna had been on the fringe of religious tradition. She believed in a form of psychic link between people and had been especially vulnerable since the tragic drowning of her son Johnnie. The possibility of being able to communicate with the dead drew her into the Spiritualist movement. The Moodies began to hold seances in their house. Interested neighbours and friends gathered around their dining-room table and held hands. Catharine attended whenever she visited, and to everyone's amazement, she received messages from the other world in foreign tongues.

This kind of suspicious activity helped John's political enemies. He was falsely accused of corruption and, unable to extricate himself from the charges, was forced to resign as sheriff in 1862. *How are we to survive?* Susanna wondered. John was sixty-four and debilitated by a stroke he'd suffered a few months earlier.

To help pay their debts, the Moodies took in boarders. Susanna liked Eliza and Julia, mulatto sisters from Jamaica. She wrote happily to Catharine that "dear Lizzie is a daughter to me in my trouble and dear little Julia does her best with her angelic voice to drive away care." Susanna was pleased when her twenty-eight-year-old son Dunbar married Eliza. The newlyweds proposed to take care of Susanna and John, with the stipulation that their Belleville home be given to Dunbar.

In his weakened state, John decided to trust his son and formally signed over the house, but Dunbar changed the plan and sold the house so he and Eliza could move to a farm in Delaware. They wanted John and Susanna to move with them, but Susanna didn't want to leave Belleville and become a Yankee in her old age. The twenty-year stability Susanna and John had known was at an end. The other Moodie children, except for Robert, the youngest, turned against their parents. Katie and her husband John Vickers were especially bitter. They had come to the financial aid of Susanna and John in the past, and had counselled them against signing the house over to Dunbar and Eliza.

Homeless, the Moodies wondered where they could live now.

∞

Susanna quickly adapted to the small cottage they rented a mile outside Belleville, on the Bay of Quinte. From her window, she could see schooners on the lake and what she described as a "fine common with noble trees." To help pay for the wages of their servant Margaret, Susanna sold paintings she'd done of the wild roses and irises in the garden. She also kept a vegetable patch of cabbages, pumpkins, beans and potatoes. Friends visited with baskets of apples and precious tea, which Susanna admitted she couldn't do without. They kept a cow for milk and twenty-four hens for eggs.

Despite her failing eyes and the aches and pains of old age, Susanna picked up her pen to write down fables and legends she had heard as a child in Suffolk. She entitled this manuscript *The World Before Them*, and Richard Bentley published it in three volumes in 1867. When Bentley learned of their destitute state, he arranged for Susanna to receive a prestigious award from the Royal Literary Fund. Susanna cherished the embossed letter that named her as the recipient of sixty pounds, which helped to cover necessities.

In 1868, John Lovell in Montreal agreed to print John Moodie's book *Scenes and Adventures of a Soldier and Settler, During Half a Century.* The agreement stipulated that Moodie would have to sell the copies himself. Recovered from the effects of his stroke, John travelled the colony to sell books to friends and strangers. He made six hundred dollars, a feast during famine years.

∽

In July 1865, the Moodies boarded the train at the Belleville station, then switched to a stagecoach bound for Lakefield, the town north of Peterborough that Samuel Strickland had helped establish. They stayed at Samuel's comfortable mansion, the Homestead, and also at Catharine's cottage nearby. Thomas Traill had died on June 21, 1859. He had lost the will to live after Oaklands, the family house, had burned to the ground and the Traills had been forced to live on the charity of family and friends.

After twenty-six years, Susanna marvelled at how Lakefield, busy with sawmills, had flourished. She didn't recognize Main Street, with its pretty houses and gardens. Christ Anglican Church was one among several imposing churches. People hailed her and John as they walked on the new wooden sidewalk, but Susanna didn't recognize anyone. Her memory had weakened.

One morning, the couple travelled a mile out of Lakefield to their former bush property on Lake Katchewanooka. On the way, Susanna wondered, *How will it feel to return to the place where we struggled as pioneers for seven years?* She found their log cabin was gone, and all the land they had cleared had become a cedar swamp. The only visible sign of the past was the stones from their well. As Susanna stood by the edge of the lake where she had often fished for her starving children, she realized, *I am a stranger here.*

In 1864, Susanna learned that her ninety-two-year-old mother had died peacefully at Reydon Hall. Then, in 1867, her brother Samuel died of diabetes. Two years later, Susanna had an even deeper loss to face.

On October 21, 1869, after a quiet evening sitting by the parlour stove, Susanna helped John to bed. She went to rest on the couch nearby, and dozed off. She awakened suddenly, her heart beating very fast. John was calling out for her. When Susanna came to his side, she knew something was terribly wrong for John could barely speak and slurred his words. She rushed into the hallway and cried out to the maid, "Get the doctor!" She returned to John's bedside.

"I need some air," John stammered with difficulty.

Susanna wrapped a blanket around her seventy-two-year-old husband and half-carried him to the chair by the window. She opened the window wide to let the cool autumn air rush in, but soon the room was icy, so she closed the window and helped John back into bed. Susanna was afraid. *Why does the doctor live so far away? John is suffering another stroke. Will it be fatal this time?*

"Please talk to me," she pleaded, but John could only swallow hard and stare at her. At dawn, he passed away in her arms as the mill bell tolled.

∞

Robert Moodie arrived by train to help his mother with the funeral arrangements. He was accompanied by his sister Agnes and his brother-in-law John Vickers, who set aside his resentment to come to Susanna's aid in their common loss.

As she prepared for the church service, Susanna took a moment to gather her strength and went to sit in the parlour where she had spent her last happy evening with John. She could still picture him in the chair by the stove, reading to her as she knitted. How beautiful he'd looked with his silky white hair touching his shoulders. The lamp had illumined his noble features with a bright glow that gave his cheek the bloom of youth. She recalled his words as she helped him to bed – "God bless you" – and felt comforted.

The funeral procession from the Moodies' cottage to St. Thomas Anglican Church was long and included some of John's former enemies and many more of his friends. At the gravesite, Susanna wept as the coffin was lowered into the earth. How would she live without the man who had been her closest ally for nearly four decades?

11

Legacy

> Canada has become almost as dear to me as
> my native land; and the homesickness that
> constantly preyed upon me in the
> Backwoods, has long ago yielded to the
> deepest and most heartfelt interest in the
> rapidly increasing prosperity and greatness
> of the country of my adoption.
> – Susanna Moodie, *Life in the Clearings*

S usanna was homeless again. As a widow, she
couldn't afford to remain in the cottage on her own.
She was offered several places to live: Catharine
encouraged her to come to stay at her home in
Lakefield; Katie and John Vickers wanted Susanna to

Portrait of Vickers family.
Susanna lived out her last difficult days in comfort with her eldest
daughter, Katie, and Katie's husband John Vickers
in their Toronto mansion.

move to their Toronto mansion; Dunbar and Eliza pressured her to come to Delaware. But Susanna preferred to move in with her youngest son, Robert, who was her favourite. He lived with his wife Nellie in Seaforth, a town thirty-seven kilometres northwest of Toronto, where he was a station master on the Grand Trunk Railway.

It wasn't the best decision. The wooden house was cramped and shook violently each time the train came through town. Susanna liked her daughter-in-law and her three grandchildren, but she often exchanged harsh words with Mrs. Russell, Nellie's mother, who also lived in the house. Susanna couldn't tolerate how severe Mrs. Russell was with the children. Susanna retreated to her own room, which had paper-thin walls. She missed John deeply. Who could understand her as he had? Who could she talk to about everything? No one. Resourceful as ever, Susanna fended off loneliness by writing letters to Catharine, Katie, and Donald, as well as to various nephews and nieces.

After a few months, she decided to return to Belleville. She rented a room in a boarding house run by a Quaker couple. She made a daily pilgrimage to the downtown cemetery where John was buried beside their two boys, John Junior and George Arthur. There, Susanna found some relief from her sadness, and the pain in her stomach lessened. She was so tired of the liver and fish they served at the boarding house, but she knew she had to eat to stay strong. Didn't she have plans to write again? She also wanted to find a publisher for the final manuscript John had been at work on, a record of his experiences as sheriff.

Crocuses peeked out of the ground by John's grave, and Susanna felt the warm breeze embrace her.

∞

Susanna sat at her desk to write the Preface for the first Canadian edition of *Roughing It in the Bush*. She'd been approached by the Toronto firm of Hunter, Rose, and Company, who wanted to produce a reprint, and pleased by this request, she had agreed. But had she made a mistake? Her powers of concentration seemed to have left her. How she missed John, who always encouraged her to just, "Begin, dear Susie, begin and it will be good." Susanna closed her burning eyes. This Preface was aimed at Canadians, whom she had offended once already with this book. What could she say now? Susanna decided to write a letter to Katie. Her eldest daughter, the apple of John's eye, would surely be willing to help her in this matter.

In 1872, Susanna received some of the recognition she had longed for when Canadian reviewers lauded the new edition of *Roughing It in the Bush*. In her introductory chapter Susanna praised the new nation, the Dominion of Canada. Her vision of a prosperous Canada had come true. She claimed that her love for this country had steadily increased, from year to year, and her attachment to Canada was now so strong she couldn't imagine anything short of absolute necessity inducing her to return to England.

Katie had helped Susanna write about current politics. Susanna lauded the social freedom in Canada, especially for the poor, who were not ostracized as they were in England. After forty years, she still felt she had to defend her point of view in writing *Roughing It*: "I gave the experience of the first seven years we passed in the woods, attempting to clear a bush farm, as a warning to others, and the number of persons who have since told me that my book "told the history" of their own life in the woods ought to be the best proof to every candid mind that I spoke the truth."

Susanna even made money from the sale of the Canadian edition. Her son-in-law John Vickers helped her manage her finances. Katie and John knew how unhappy she was in the Belleville boarding house, and they wanted her to move into their home in Toronto. Instead, Susanna accepted Catharine's invitation to live with her at Westove.

Westove was Catharine's charming cottage in Lakefield. Susanna had a pretty bedroom on the second floor, with its own woodstove. She was happy that she had full use of the kitchen and could fetch herself a piece of bread with butter anytime she liked, which she had been unable to do in the boarding house. From her window, Susanna heard the waves on Lake Katchewanooka. In the summer, Catherine's garden bloomed with roses and delphiniums. Susanna liked to sit there and rest in a comfortable chair for hours. She rarely went to the village, which was only a ten-minute walk. This idyllic life was completely different from the hardships she'd endured in the bush cabin only a mile away four decades earlier.

Susanna enjoyed writing light verse to entertain
her grandchildren. In 1876, she sent these lines to her
nephew William Vickers, who'd lost his mittens:
Now here me Billie, I will declare
I will not knit you another pair!
I'll leave it to younger hands than mine,
To keep warm that heart and hand of thine,
When I take up the pins in your behalf
I give you leave my boy to laugh –
At old Knitty Knotty, who loves you well,
And hopes to see you a learned swell…
She suffered from a lack of privacy at Westove
since gregarious Catharine encouraged family and
friends to visit at any time. Susanna grew tired of the
constant commotion and wanted to move again.

In 1874, Agnes Strickland died. Susanna mourned the
elder sister who had hurt her so deeply years earlier,
but whom she had forgiven. They had resumed writing
to each other when Agnes had offered her condolences
at the death of John. Susanna had always looked up to
Agnes and admired her theatrical and literary talent.
When Susanna read the obituary in the Toronto *Globe*
and noticed errors, she complained to the editor and
added her own magnanimous tribute:
"Space will not permit me to say more of this truly
great woman. Her genius is too well appreciated to
need it…(She was) an affectionate, loving daughter, a
faithful sister and friend, kind and benevolent to the
poor, and possessing warm sympathies for the sick and

suffering; she never let the adulation of the world interfere with the blessed domestic charities."

Susanna felt Agnes's stinginess beyond the grave when she was excluded from her sister's will, receiving not even a memento. Catharine was bequeathed the copyright to the *Lives of the Queens of England*, which brought her much-needed money.

In 1877, Susanna lived once again with Robert and Nellie and their children, though she was spared the presence of Nellie's cantankerous mother, Mrs. Russell. One afternoon, in their downtown Toronto house on Wilton Crescent, Susanna entertained an unexpected guest, who brought back a flood of memories from Suffolk. His name was James Ewing Ritchie, the son of Reverend Andrew Ritchie. James told her he had been commissioned by the London periodical the *Christian World* to interview British emigrants who lived in Canada. Susanna poured him a second cup of tea and continued to reminisce, as Ritchie took notes. He could barely keep up with all the anecdotes that Susanna recounted of her childhood. It struck him that the author had retained in old age the enthusiasm for which she was remarkable when young.

James Ritchie also visited Catharine in Lakefield and found her equally remarkable. Ritchie was the first to describe the Strickland sisters as "pioneers of Canadian literature" in his book *To Canada with Emigrants*.

∞

At eighty-one, Susanna was feeble. She couldn't walk without assistance, she couldn't concentrate to read, couldn't even distinguish between her children and grandchildren. Susanna moved to Katie and John's stone mansion on Adelaide Street where there was more room and tranquility, and where a full-time nurse could be accommodated. John Vickers was the only member of the family who had made money, successfully building his own delivery company, the Vickers Northern Express. He not only supported Katie and their ten children in comfort, but also helped other members of the family like Susanna.

Catharine came for a visit and was shocked at her younger sister's deterioration of mind and body. In her bedroom, Susanna sat in a chair holding in her arms a big wax doll. Catharine thought this eerie, for Susanna had rejected dolls all her life, had called them "idols," and had even refused to give any to her daughters. Catharine remembered how Susanna preferred live pets. She remembered how at Reydon Hall, Susanna had hidden a lizard in her pinafore, cooing at it and calling it her "beautiful darling," until their nursemaid, horrified, had taken it away from her.

On Easter morning, Susanna's state of mind became even more alarming to her sister. When Susanna heard the church bells ring, she mumbled that it was for the murderer who had cut off her head, and fell down on her knees to pray for him. Susanna suffered from dementia. Catharine immediately changed her plans: she wouldn't return to Lakefield yet; she would stay by her ailing sister's side. Susanna fell into a coma, and she died thirty-six hours later, on April 8, 1885.

Photo by Gerry Boyce. Hastings County Historical Society Archives, Belleville, Ontario.

In the cemetery by the waters of the Bay of Quinte, Belleville,
stands a marble angel holding a star,
in memory of Susanna Moodie.

EPILOGUE

The Dark Angel

Who can read the Poet's dream...
The upward soaring of a soul
Unfettered by the world's control
Onward, heavenward ever tending,
Its essence with the eternal blending...
— Susanna Moodie, *The Poet*

K atie Moodie Vickers, the sturdy, dark-haired eldest
daughter of Susanna, deposited a wreath of roses
and ivy at her mother's grave in the Belleville cemetery.
The waters of the Bay of Quinte shone in the distance
in the warm autumn sunshine. John Vickers, a man
with a sharp nose and bushy beard, admired the monu-
ment he had commissioned in the memory of his

mother-in-law. It had cost a lot of money, but Katie wanted the best for her mother, and so did he. Together, they looked at the life-size marble angel: the wings were open wide, the head held high, and in one hand, there was a star. John Vickers thought how Susanna had been a star that shone bright in their lives, and in the lives of the readers of her works – certainly her most celebrated, *Roughing It in the Bush*. In fact, the family had been touched to read the long obituary in the Toronto *Globe*, which said, among other complimentary statements, that Mrs. Moodie had been a Canadian author of the best-read book in Canada. John Vickers was an Irishman, born in Dublin, and he knew from first-hand experience that being an immigrant was a difficult life. Susanna had captured the pioneer experience for future generations.

Katie didn't remember emigrating, for she had come to Canada as a baby in the arms of her mother. In life, her mother had been like a dark angel, hovering over her family but preoccupied with her own dreams and visions. How often Katie had done the chores so her mother could write the stories that she needed to tell the world. Susanna had felt passionate about her adopted country and had envisioned from its early beginnings that it would be a great nation. Beside Susanna lay John Moodie, who had shared her passion for writing and for Canada, and had been the best of fathers.

"Are you ready to go, my dear?" her husband asked.

Katie looked tenderly at the man who had given her and their ten children such a comfortable life and generously helped her family when they were in trouble. She took his arm, and they walked away from the gravesite, to go back home.

Afterword

Susanna Moodie became famous again in Canada in the early 1970s with the publication of Margaret Atwood's award-winning collection, *The Journals of Susanna Moodie*. Atwood claimed that Moodie had appeared to her in a dream, which inspired the cycle of haunting poems.

That is how I first came to read about Susanna Moodie, pioneer author. I sought out a copy of *Roughing It in the Bush*, which I found to be a roughly crafted book filled with a visionary female spirit.

Moodie has influenced other contemporary Canadian authors. Timothy Findley and Carol Shields both used Moodie as a character in their fiction. And Shields wrote a book of criticism, *Susanna Moodie: Voice & Vision*, in which she remarked that the nineteenth-century author was a "bridging figure" who struggled "between the tug of tradition and the pull of progress."

It was soon after finishing *Sisters in the Wilderness*, Charlotte Gray's 1999 bestseller about Catharine Parr Traill and Susanna Moodie, that I was offered the opportunity to write for the Quest Library Series. Gray's brilliantly researched biography, as well as Michael Peterman's meticulous editing of Moodie's correspondence, *Letters of a Lifetime*, were important sources for my own version of Moodie's life.

As I wrote each draft of her dramatic story, my own life was marked by major loss and illnesses, but I never wanted to abandon this project. In fact, I believe Susanna's invincible spirit gave me strength to go on.

I want to thank Terry Rigelhof for his suggestion that I write a Quest Library biography and his faith in my ability to do so in spite of my troubles. I want to thank Rhonda Bailey for her enthusiastic response to my choice of subject, namely Susanna Moodie, and for her editorial expertise. And a special thanks to Cynthia Cecil and Munira Judith Avinger.

I also want to thank Karen Raymond and Catherine Hobbs at Library and Archives Canada in Ottawa for their gracious assistance. At the library, I had the privilege of slipping on a pair of pristine white gloves to handle precious original documents, letters, books, and even paintings by Susanna Moodie.

Chronology of Susanna Moodie (1803-1885)

Compiled by Clarence Karr

SUSANNA MOODIE AND HER TIMES	CANADA AND THE WORLD
	1791 The British Constitutional (Canada) Act creates Upper Canada and Lower Canada, the future provinces of Ontario and Quebec.
	1794 Richard Bentley, a future publisher, is born in England.
1797 John Dunbar Moodie, future husband of Susanna, is born in the Orkney Islands, Scotland.	
	1798 William Wordsworth and Samuel Taylor Coleridge publish *Lyrical Ballads*.

SUSANNA MOODIE AND HER TIMES	CANADA AND THE WORLD
1802	**1802**
Catharine Parr Strickland, older sister of Susanna, is born.	Napoleon Bonaparte is confirmed as consul of France for life. He creates the Legion of Honour to replace royal titles.
1803	**1803**
Susanna Strickland is born in the village of Bungay, Suffolk, England. She is the sixth daughter of Elizabeth Homer and Thomas Strickland.	Chief Justice William Osgoode of Lower Canada rules slavery to be inconsistent with British law.
	Britain declares war on France.
	Beethoven dedicates his Third Symphony (*Eroica*) to Napoleon.
	The United States buys the Louisiana Purchase from France, effectively doubling its territory.
1804	**1804**
Susanna's brother Samuel is born.	Napoleon is crowned Emperor of France in Notre Dame Cathedral. The Code Napoleon is adopted as French Civil law. Many other countries of the world will adopt this legal framework.
	1807
	In western North America, David Thompson of the North West Company crosses the Rocky Mountains and establishes Kootenai House, the first fur-trading post in what is now southeastern British Columbia. Thompson is already a legendary map-maker of the British North American fur-trading west.

SUSANNA MOODIE AND HER TIMES

CANADA AND THE WORLD

1808

Five-year-old Susanna moves with her family to the Elizabethan manor Reydon Hall on the Suffolk coast.

1808

Sir Guy Carleton (Lord Dorchester), second governor of British Quebec, dies.

Napoleon invades Spain. His army encounters its first serious resistance.

1810

Susanna's parents provide her and her sisters with a solid education, including some Latin and Greek. Her father's library provides ample opportunity for extensive reading. Her favourite authors include Sir Walter Scott with his medieval and Scottish heroes. Napoleon is one of her contemporary heroes.

1810

John Lovell, a future printer and publisher, is born in County Cork, Ireland.

Napoleon's marriage to Josephine is annulled and he marries Marie-Louise of Austria.

King George III of Britain is recognized as insane. A regency period follows with his son serving as the monarch.

1811

David Thompson reaches the mouth of the Columbia River to find the American Pacific Fur Co. already there. He travels up the full length of the Columbia.

1815

Twelve-year-old Susanna is writing poetry and drama.

1815

Napoleon escapes from captivity on the island of Elba. European forces defeat him for the final time at the Battle of Waterloo, which creates a British hero, the Duke of Wellington.

John A. Macdonald, who will become the first prime minister of Canada, is born in Scotland.

SUSANNA MOODIE AND HER TIMES	CANADA AND THE WORLD
	1816 Lord Byron publishes *Childe Harold's Pilgrimage*. Charlotte Brontë is born.
1818 Susanna's father Thomas Strickland dies, leaving his family with little capital. Circumstances encourage the Strickland daughters to supplement the family income by writing.	**1818** John Keats publishes *Endymion*; Mary Shelley publishes *Frankenstein*; Sir Walter Scott publishes *Rob Roy*. The forty-ninth parallel becomes the border between the United States and the British Hudson's Bay Company's trading territory from the Lake of the Woods to the Rocky Mountains.
1819 Susanna visits London for the first time. She stays at her "aunt" Rebecca Leverton's home in Bedford Square.	
	1820 Ten-year-old John Lovell emigrates from Ireland to Lower Canada with his family. In Britain, King George III dies and is succeeded by his son, George IV.
1825 Susanna's younger brother, Samuel Strickland, emigrates to Upper Canada.	**1825** Peter Robinson brings 2,000 poor Irish settlers to what will become the Peterborough area of Upper Canada in an assisted emigration experiment.

SUSANNA MOODIE
AND HER TIMES

CANADA AND THE WORLD

The Canada Land Company is formed by John Galt and other Scottish investors to settle British emigrants in Upper Canada.

Scottish factory owner Robert Owen buys 30,000 acres in Indiana as the site for New Harmony utopian community.

1826

Susanna lives in London for a few months at the home of her cousin Thomas Cheesman. He probably paints her miniature portrait (and Catharine's) at this time.

1828

Susanna befriends Thomas Pringle as they work for the Anti-Slavery Society. Recently arrived from South Africa, he encourages Susanna's writing. He asks her to ghost write the stories of two West Indian slaves for publication.

1828

John James Audubon's first volume of the ten-volume *The Birds of America* is published.

The Duke of Wellington becomes prime minister of Britain.

The Canada Land Company creates the community of Stratford in Upper Canada.

1829

Susanna wins praise for her published story "Old Hanna: or, The Charm" based on the family's old, cantankerous servant.

1829

Future Canadian publisher George MacLean Rose is born in Wick, Scotland.

Upper Canada College is founded in Toronto.

The first Welland Canal opens, allowing ship traffic between Lake

SUSANNA MOODIE AND HER TIMES	CANADA AND THE WORLD
	Ontario and Lake Erie for the first time.
1830 Susanna becomes a convert to the Congregationalist Church, the English Calvinist church. The switch away from the Church of England shocks her family.	**1830** Greece frees itself from Ottoman Turkish rule.
	Belgium wins its independence from the Netherlands.
While staying as a guest at the Pringles', Susanna meets John Dunbar Moodie. He is a retired officer on a small pension who has recently returned from South Africa.	English author Alfred Tennyson publishes *Poems Chiefly Lyrical*.
	In France, a revolution deposes the Bourbon king, Charles X. Louis Philippe becomes "citizen" king.
	The American congress passes the Indian Removal Act.
1831 After John Dunbar Moodie abandons his plans to return to South Africa, Susanna agrees to marry him. She publishes *Enthusiasm and Other Poems* by private subscription. The two anti-slavery tracts she has ghost-written are also published: *Negro Slavery Described by a Negro* and *The History of Mary Prince, a West Indian Slave.*	**1831** Charles Darwin embarks on his world journey on the H.M.S. *Beagle*.
	The Russian army takes the Polish capital of Warsaw. Composer Frederic Chopin escapes to Paris.
1832 Susanna's sister Catharine Parr marries Thomas Traill. They emigrate to Upper Canada.	**1832** Sir Walter Scott dies. Tennyson publishes *The Lady of Shallot*. Frances Trollope publishes her critical and satirical *Domestic Manners of the Americans*.

SUSANNA MOODIE AND HER TIMES

Susanna gives birth to a baby girl, which she and John name Catherine (Katie).

John and Susanna Moodie follow her sister and brother-in-law to Upper Canada in hopes of improving their financial prospects. They purchase a cleared farm near Cobourg.

1833
Susanna publishes stories in the *Albion* magazine in New York City.

She gives birth to a second daughter named Agnes.

1834
The Moodies move to another farm north of Peterborough in an area closer to her brother Samuel and the Traills.

Susanna gives birth to her first son, John Alexander Dunbar.

While her husband John is away, a fire in the fallow threatens to burn the house with Susanna, her children, and the servants trapped inside.

1835
The London firm of Richard Bentley publishes J. W. Dunbar Moodie's *Ten Years in South Africa*.

CANADA AND THE WORLD

The western world's first cholera epidemic spreads from Europe and is carried by emigrant ships to North America. Several thousand Canadians succumb.

1833
The British parliament passes the Slavery Abolition Act to provide an end to slavery the following year throughout the British Empire.

1834
York is incorporated as the city of Toronto. William Lyon Mackenzie is elected mayor.

A new British Poor Law comes into effect providing for charity only in workhouses.

Samuel Taylor Coleridge dies.

1835
Hans Christian Andersen publishes his first book of fairy tales.

1836

Catharine Parr Traill publishes *The Backwoods of Canada* with a London firm, Charles Knight. It is in a genre of emigration literature that informs and encourages.

Susanna gives birth to a second son, Donald.

1836

Charles Dickens agrees to edit Richard Bentley's new magazine, *Bentley's Miscellany*.

Spain recognizes the independence of Mexico.

1837

In early December John Dunbar Moodie answers the call for militia volunteers to defend Upper Canada from the rebels.

Susanna has a second terrifying experience with fire when the cabin roof catches fire.

1837

Rebellions against British rule break out in Lower and Upper Canada. The Toronto revolt is led by William Lyon Mackenzie. A defeated Mackenzie flees to the United States.

Eighteen-year-old Victoria becomes Queen of Britain and the Empire.

Samuel Morse patents the telegraph.

1838

John Dunbar Moodie spends much of the year away on militia duty. Alone on the farm, a pregnant Susanna is lonely and depressed. Some of her patriotic poems are published in Upper Canadian newspapers. She also begins to submit work to the *Literary Garland*.

Later this year a third son, John Strickland, is born. The Moodies nickname him Johnnie.

1838

Charles Dickens serializes *Oliver Twist* in *Bentley's Miscellany*.

John Lovell and his brother-in-law John Gibson establish the *Literary Garland* in Montreal. This will be the Canadas' first successful literary magazine as well as the first to pay contributors.

Susanna Moodie and Her Times	Canada and the World
1839 John Dunbar Moodie is appointed sheriff of the Victoria district.	**1839** Louis Daguerre creates the world's first photographic process, which will be named daguerreotype.
1840 The Moodie family moves to the town of Belleville. Susanna becomes a regular contributor to the *Literary Garland*. Susanna gives birth to another son, George Arthur, who dies within weeks. A fire in the Moodie cottage in Belleville takes most of their belongings, but no one is hurt. They move to a house on Bridge Street, along the Moira River.	**1840** After establishing the uniform penny post, Britain inaugurates the world's first postage stamp. Queen Victoria marries Prince Albert of Saxe Coburg-Gotha. May Fleming, future Canadian popular novelist is born
1841 Susanna's literary reputation grows. She establishes contact with other writers and meets publisher John Lovell.	**1841** Upper and Lower Canada are united into one colony, the Canadas. For a short period Kingston becomes the capital. Queen Victoria grants a royal charter to Queen's University in the new capital.
1843 Susanna gives birth to another boy, named Robert Baldwin after the Toronto-based leader of the Reform party.	**1843** In Canada, Grace Marks is convicted of murdering her employer and his housekeeper. David Thompson completes work on an atlas that maps the land

SUSANNA MOODIE AND HER TIMES	CANADA AND THE WORLD
	from Hudson's Bay to the Pacific, an area of 3.9 million sq. km.
	The first amusement park, Tivoli Gardens, opens in Copenhagen, Denmark.
1844 The Moodies' six-year-old son Johnnie drowns in the Moira River.	**1844** The first electric telegraph is sent by Samuel Morse from Baltimore to Washington saying, "What God hath Wrought."
1847 Susanna and John edit and contribute much of the material to the short-lived *Victoria Magazine*.	**1847** The St. Lawrence River canal system is completed.
	A continuing potato famine in Ireland causes the death of many. Thousands also emigrate to North America and Australia.
	In Britain, Emily Brontë publishes *Wuthering Heights*.
1849 Susanna visits Kingston Penitentiary and meets notorious murderer Grace Marks.	**1849** Lord Elgin, Governor of the Canadas, signs the Rebellion Losses Bill signalling the functioning of responsible government in the colony. The signing prompts a riot in Montreal, and the building in which the legislature was meeting is burned.
	William Lyon Mackenzie is pardoned and returns to Canada from the U.S.

SUSANNA MOODIE AND HER TIMES

CANADA AND THE WORLD

Harriet Tubman escapes to the northern American states and begins working with an underground railway to forward escaped slaves north to the British colonies. Quakers play a prominent role in this phenomenon by providing safe houses.

1851
The *Literary Garland* ceases publication.

Publisher George MacLean Rose emigrates from Scotland to Montreal, Canada East.

William Lyon Mackenzie is elected to the Legislative Assembly of Upper Canada, but he no longer has a power base or influence.

1852
Richard Bentley publishes Susanna Moodie's *Roughing It in the Bush.* He supplies her with the current literature from Britain by such authors as Tennyson, Thackeray, Dickens, and Longfellow.

Susanna visits Niagara Falls, which she will feature in her next book.

Catharine Parr Traill publishes a children's book, *Canadian Crusoes.*

1853
Bentley publishes Susanna Moodie's memoir *Life in the*

1852
Harriet Beecher Stowe publishes *Uncle Tom's Cabin.* It will be a long-term best-seller in both North America and Europe. This novel becomes the first work of fiction to sell more than a million copies in Britain.

A fire in Montreal burns 11,000 houses.

1853
Charles Dickens publishes *Bleak House*; Elizabeth Gaskell pub-

Clearings versus the Bush. He also publishes collected fictional pieces from the *Literary Garland* and her novel *Mark Hurdlestone: the gold worshipper*.

Susanna's brother Samuel publishes a memoir, *Twenty-Seven Years in Canada West*.

lishes *Ruth*; and Charles Kingsley publishes *Hypatia*.

A railway opens between Portland, Maine and Montreal. This international line provides the Canadas with their first ice-free port.

1854
Bentley publishes Moodie's autobiographical novel *Flora Lyndsay: or Passages in an Eventful Life*.

1854
The Crimean War begins when Britain, France, and Turkey declare war on Russia.

Alfred Tennyson publishes *The Charge of the Light Brigade*. Florence Nightingale departs from England for the war zone with thirty-eight nurses.

1855
Susanna Moodie publishes a novel, *Geoffrey Moncton: or, the faithless guardian*, with the U.S. firm Dewitt and Davenport.

The Moodies receive a visit from famed American Spiritualist Kate Fox, formerly of Belleville.

Catharine Parr Traill's *The Canadian Settler's Guide* appears from a Toronto publisher.

1855
British forces defeat the Russians at Sevastopol.

H.W. Longfellow publishes the *Song of Hiawatha*.

Walt Whitman publishes *Leaves of Grass*.

1856
John Dunbar Moodie visits the Fox sisters in New York City. None of the family's Spiritualist

1856
George Eliot publishes *Adam Bede*; Anthony Trollope, *Barchester Towers*; and W. M. Thackeray, *The Virginians*.

SUSANNA MOODIE AND HER TIMES	CANADA AND THE WORLD

sessions result in contact with their drowned son Johnnie.

1859
Thomas Traill dies.

1859
Erastus Beadle publishes *The Dime Book of Practical Etiquette.*

1861
In January, Abraham Lincoln becomes president of the United States. Seven states secede from the Union and form a confederacy. By April, four more states have joined the Confederacy. Jefferson Davis becomes President of the Confederated States of America.

The American Civil War officially begins at Fort Sumter, South Carolina on 12 April.

The American army abolishes flogging.

1862
John Dunbar Moodie suffers a stroke and is forced to resign as sheriff. Susanna takes in boarders to pay the bills.

Due to a misunderstanding with their son Dunbar, the Moodies lose their house on Bridge Street and are forced to rent a small cottage on the Bay of Quinte.

1862
The American Civil War continues.

The first female student is accepted by Mount Allison University in Sackville, New Brunswick.

1864
Susanna's ninety-two-year-old mother dies in England.

1864
The Fathers of Confederation meet in successive conferences at

SUSANNA MOODIE AND HER TIMES	CANADA AND THE WORLD

John Lovell publishes *Selections from Canadian Poets*, edited by Edward Hartley Dewart. It includes poems by Moodie, Alexander McLachlan, Charles Sangster, and others.

Charlottetown and Quebec City. They agree on the principles of a constitution for a new nation.

With a victory of the American army over the Southern Confederates at Gettysburg, the tide of the war turns in favour of the North.

Alfred Tennyson publishes *Enoch Arden*.

1865
In April, U.S. President Abraham Lincoln is assassinated. The Civil War ends. In January, the ratification of the Thirteenth Amendment to the Constitution of the United States abolishes slavery.

1867
Susanna's brother Samuel Strickland dies. Richard Bentley publishes Susanna's *The World Before Them*. It recounts fables and legends from her childhood in Suffolk.

1867
Canadians celebrate the birth of their nation on July 1. Canadian Confederation unites Ontario, Quebec, Nova Scotia, and New Brunswick. John A. Macdonald becomes the first prime minister and is knighted by Queen Victoria. Ottawa becomes capital of the new Confederation.

1868
Agnes Fitzgibbon and Catharine Parr Traill publish *Canadian Wild Flowers*.

1868
Canadian politician Thomas D'Arcy McGee is assassinated.

Louisa May Alcott publishes *Little Women*.

SUSANNA MOODIE AND HER TIMES	CANADA AND THE WORLD
1869 John Dunbar Moodie dies. Homeless, Susanna lives for a time with her youngest son Robert and his wife near Toronto, then moves to a boarding house in Belleville.	**1869** In the Red River Rebellion led by Louis Riel, the Métis people resist the terms of the transfer of the Red River settlement to Canada and negotiate the terms of the entry of a new province, Manitoba, into Confederation, which becomes official the following year.
1871 The Toronto firm of Hunter, Rose, and Company publishes the first Canadian edition of *Roughing It in The Bush*. Susanna adds a preface praising the new Dominion of Canada.	**1871** Richard Bentley dies. John Lovell publishes the massive *Canadian Dominion Directory*. At 2,562 pages it was the largest volume ever published in Canada. British Columbia joins Canada as the sixth province.
1872 Susanna goes to live with her sister Catharine at Lakefield.	**1872** Publisher George MacLean Rose and his partner Robert Hunter establish the *Canadian Monthly and National Review*, which will include works by Alexander Begg, Alexander McLachlan, and other Canadian authors. **1873** Prince Edward Island joins Confederation.
1874 Susanna's elder sister Agnes dies.	**1874** L.M. Montgomery is born.

SUSANNA MOODIE AND HER TIMES	CANADA AND THE WORLD
1875	**1875**
Susanna's work appears in the *Canadian Monthly and National Review*.	Alexander Graham Bell travels to Washington to file a patent for the telephone.
	The first organized game of indoor ice hockey is played in Montreal at the Victoria Skating Rink.
	Danish writer Hans Christian Andersen and English novelist Charles Kingsley die.
1877	**1877**
Susanna moves to Toronto to live with her son Robert and his wife.	The British parliament passes the Royal Titles Act, which proclaims Queen Victoria as Empress of India.
	Following the pyrrhic victory in the Battle of the Little Big Horn, Chief Sitting Bull leads his Dakota band north into Canada to escape from the American army.
1884	**1884**
Susanna now lives with her eldest daughter, Katie, Katie's husband John Vickers, and their ten children. The Vickers have a large home in Toronto. Susanna needs a full-time nurse in attendance.	The siege of Khartoum begins with the local Mahdi against the British led by General Charles George Gordon, the Governor of the Sudan.
	The first edition of the *Oxford English Dictionary* appears.
1885	**1885**
Susanna Moodie dies on April 8 and is buried in Belleville, Ontario.	The Northwest Rebellion breaks out on the Canadian prairie. Rebel leader Louis Riel is captured, tried, and executed. The Canadian Pacific Railway is completed.

**SUSANNA MOODIE
AND HER TIMES**

CANADA AND THE WORLD

The siege of Khartoum ends with the defeat of the British and the death of General Gordon. Popular indignation in Britain helps to cause the downfall of the government of William Gladstone.

W.S. Gilbert and Arthur Sullivan launch *The Mikado*.

1896
Wilfrid Laurier, a Liberal, is elected prime minister of Canada. He is the first French Canadian to assume the office.

1897
Queen Victoria celebrates her Diamond Jubilee. Canadian Prime Minister Wilfrid Laurier is knighted by the Queen.

The Klondike Gold Rush begins. American author Jack London sails north to the goldfields where he will write his first successful stories.

1898
Canadian publisher George MacLean Rose dies.

The USS *Maine* explodes and sinks in the harbour of Havana, Cuba. With a declaration of war by the United States against Spain, the Spanish-American War begins.

SUSANNA MOODIE AND HER TIMES	**CANADA AND THE WORLD**
1899 Catharine Parr Traill dies in Lakefield, Ontario.	**1899** The Boer War begins in South Africa. French-Canadian cabinet member in the Laurier government Henri Bourassa reigns to protest Canada's involvement. Approximately 2,000 Doukhobors arrive in Halifax to settle in Canada. They are fleeing from Russia to escape Czarist repression.
1914 A new edition of Susanna Moodie's *Roughing It in the Bush* reaches tenth position on the Canadian bestseller list.	**1914** The First World War begins. After training at Valcartier, the first Canadian troops depart for England. Canadian author Stephen Leacock publishes *Arcadian Adventures of the Idle Rich*. The Panama Canal opens to traffic. **1927** A struggling Canadian writer, Mazo de la Roche, wins the *Atlantic Monthly*-Little Brown Award of $10,000 for her novel *Jalna*.
1962 McClelland and Stewart issue a paperback edition of *Roughing It in the Bush* in the New Canadian Library series. The book becomes an important fixture in the prolif-	**1962** John Glenn becomes the first American to orbit the earth in space.

Susanna Moodie and Her Times	Canada and the World
erating Canadian literature courses in universities.	Pope John XXIII convenes the Second Vatican Council, the first in ninety-two years.

1965

Carl Ballstadt completes a PhD thesis for the University of London on "The literary history of the Strickland family."

1965

The United States sends the first combat troops to Vietnam.

The Beatles release the song "Love Me Do."

1966

Clara Thomas writes of Susanna and Catharine Strickland in *The Clear Spirit: Twenty Canadian Women and Their Times*.

1966

The Montreal Metro opens. This is the first subway transportation system in Canada.

1968

A.Y. Morris includes Susanna Moodie in her *Gentle Pioneers: Five Nineteenth-Century Canadians*.

1968

The Liberal Party led by Pierre Trudeau wins a majority government in a general election.

Martin Luther King Jr. is assassinated.

1970

Margaret Atwood publishes her award-winning cycle of poems, *The Journals of Susanna Moodie*.

1970

In Quebec, FLQ terrorists kidnap British diplomat James Cross and Quebec cabinet minister Pierre Laporte. Prime Minister Trudeau invokes the War Measures Act. Laporte is killed by his abductors.

National Guardsmen kill four students protesting the Vietnam War at Kent State University in Ohio.

1973

The Writers Union of Canada is formed "to bring writers together

SUSANNA MOODIE AND HER TIMES	CANADA AND THE WORLD
	for the advancement of their collective interests."
1976 Carol Shields publishes *Susanna Moodie: Voice & Vision*.	**1976** The Parti Québécois wins the provincial election in Québec.
	The CN Tower is completed in Toronto. It becomes the world's tallest free-standing land structure.
1985 Carl Ballstadt leads a team in preparing Susanna Moodie's letters for publication.	**1985** *The Canadian Encyclopedia* is launched.
	Rick Hansen launches his Man in Motion world tour in support of spinal cord research.
	1996 Margaret Atwood features murderess Grace Marks in her 1996 novel, *Alias Grace*.
1999 Charlotte Gray publishes *Sisters in the Wilderness*, a popular study of Susanna and Catharine Strickland.	**1999** The Euro currency is introduced.
Michael Peterman publishes *Susanna Moodie: A Life*.	

Sources Consulted

Books

ATWOOD, Margaret. *The Journals of Susanna Moodie*.Toronto: Oxford University Press, 1970.

BALLSTADT, Carl, Elizabeth HOPKINS, and Michael PETERMAN, Editors. *Susanna Moodie: Letters of a Lifetime*. Toronto: University of Toronto Press, 1985.

BERTON, Pierre. *A Picture Book of Niagara Falls*. Toronto: McCLelland and Stewart, 1993.

GRAY, Charlotte. *Sisters in the Wilderness*. Toronto: Penguin Books, 1999.

MOODIE, Susanna. *Roughing It in the Bush*. Ottawa: Tecumseh Press, 1997.

———. *Roughing It in the Bush*. Toronto: McCLelland and Stewart, 1989.

———. *Life in the Clearings versus the Bush*. Toronto: McCLelland and Stewart, 1989.

———. *Enthusiasm & Other Poems*. London: Smith and Elder, 1831.

PETERMAN, Michael. *Susanna Moodie: A Life*. Toronto: ECW Press, 1999.

SHIELDS, Carol. *Susanna Moodie: Voice & Vision*. Ottawa: Borealis Press, 1977.

TRAILL, Catherine Parr. *The Backwoods of Canada.*
   Toronto: McCLelland and Stewart, 1966.

Website

www.collectionscanada.ca (Library and Archives
   Canada)

Index